MY TURN

SOUTH AFRICA

ALICE VL

MY TURN – SOUTH AFRICA

Alice VL

MY TURN – SOUTH AFRICA

Alice VL

MY TURN – SOUTH AFRICA

Alice VL

MY TURN – SOUTH AFRICA

Give me twenty divisions of American soldiers, and I will breach Europe. Give me fifteen consisting of Englishmen, and I will advance to the borders of Berlin. Give me two divisions of those marvellous fighting Boers, and I will remove Germany from the face of the earth.

~ Field Marshal Bernard L. Montgomery

DEDICATION
WARRIOR WOMAN

With love and great respect, my first dedication goes out to a fellow warrior princess, Brandi Sheats, who has spent many hours, many days, and many sleepless nights desperately bringing the plight of our scuffed nation to the world.

She stands without uniform on a battlefield that shows no mercy for her, yet, she still chooses the right side, as treacherous as it is. As often as she is beat down, she gets up again, flicks away the ashes of the fires she is tossed into, and soldiers on. On this battlefield, she faces blindfolds around the hearts of those able to put an end to a war no-one wants to acknowledge, instead, their willful ignorance only guarantees one thing; she will fight harder and longer for those caged by fear.

Amid the chaos, she remains strong as though made from the finest steel, born from divine flames. A servant for the weak, a master for the strong and an enemy of evil. You won't see the warrior in her until you go after a nation she fell in love with. That's when it becomes her combat. That's when the line gets

Alice VL

crossed. She doesn't have super strength or laser eyes, but her bravery and courage washes through her like a perfect surfer's wave.

I am honored to fight this warfare with you. Blessed beyond measure that our paths crossed, and willing to go to war not only *with* you, but *for* you.

Alice VL

DEDICATION
The McCormack & Meyer Family

For Monty and Kennith McCormack, his fiancèe Marietjie Meyer
and her nine-year-old daughter, Kayla, and the thousands of
others who were brutally murdered for being white.

Alice VL

MY TURN – SOUTH AFRICA

Alice VL

ACKNOWLEDGEMENTS

My husband, for packing your bags, and travelling to the end of the world with me. For allowing me the one chance to try and bring help to our tribe, while patiently drying my tears when I have trouble breaking down the doors.

Duross (Hiro) Gasperi, for spending hours filing on behalf of South Africa, and asking for nothing in return. For being a button I, and my country can press on.

Vanessa Harris, for your amazing, Godly visions. For desperately fighting each day to free a nation, give them a new life, and stand behind them as they chase their liberty. For encouraging me to shake off the bad and begin again tomorrow.

My children. You are inheriting tomorrow, what we leave behind today. For you, we fight to make the world better. We will never back down. 'Die land behoort aan jou.'

RS, CJ, CZ, LK, JS, CE, DG, BS, VH – you women know who you are. Without you, I could never have gotten through this year.

Alice VL

CONTENTS

Alice VL

MY TURN – SOUTH AFRICA

DEDICATION TO MY TRIBE

The unity and love of our people, our nation cannot be lessened by emotions of hatred, fear, or power. It's time to take hands against all that fuels racism against us, and all that seeks to destroy us. It's time to take hands against a power that calls for our suffering and our death. A bitter divide has grown amongst us as our tribe continues to fuel the already harsh fires set by the others. Yet, with so much against us, so many that hate us and curse us for breathing in the wrong color, we have become our own divide leaving us increasingly vulnerable to the enemy.

It's time to take hands and call on each other for the protection of our children and our elderly, our women and our men, but more importantly, for the survival of our God and our country. Then, let them gather around us where we stand in unity and watch as we stop their bitter invasion of our culture, our heritage, and our home. It's time to take hands and form a tight circle around our nation. The numbers won't matter for our strength lies in our union.

It's time to take hands against those who are here to

Alice VL

dehumanize us and cast us in a light where we deserve the cruelty and barbaric acts against us. Between them and from the highest, they have consent to invade our minds, subduing and destroying us, while keeping us prisoners of their own fears. It's time to take hands and love our tribe without borders, unconditionally, and take back the people we were before they started carving away at our souls.

It's time to take hands and free our minds of the belief that we stand alone, and that we are guilty of crimes simply identified by the color of our skin. It's time to preserve our history and our truths, irrespective of what the others are indoctrinated to believe to be true by the false and inept leaders who tailor-make our history to suit their narratives. For, when we take hands, we once more become a nation led by God, admired by our allies, and feared by the others.

It's time to take hands for these are the days of a slow progressing combat. One waged on all of our nation as they seek to overrun our souls by impressing their truths and invoking fear. Together, and holding onto one another, we will again remain focused on who we are, who we were, and who we will become again. As a nation united, their power will dwindle, evil will be exposed. and the death and carnage won't be for nothing.

Alice VL

MY TURN – SOUTH AFRICA

It's time to take hands. We are here, on the ground while the world watches through filters as the others come for us. The world can't see how the enemy sets out to execute you, me and all of our tribe. Whatever crimes were committed in the past, they were never our crimes, yet their desire for our blood knows no bounds. From our babies to our aged, the call for their execution is loud and clear, but filtered to the world. They hunt us and are thrilled by their kills, almost as though they are collecting trophies. The screens don't show this. They don't show the sick joy of evil the others present when they come for violence and destruction.

It's time to take hands, and to remind ourselves that the others feel nothing. They feel no guilt and no remorse and have taken none of the peace that was once offered by our tribe. Still, taking one another's hands will become the walls, barriers, and our safety during our storms. Our unity will be our strength, and it will come from our love of our God, and our country. It's time to place your hand in mine, feel our hearts beat stronger while our forgotten pride for our nation grows fiercer. We are accountable for each other; it has always been our gift to our tribe. It's time to take hands as we command our nation, and our legion. United, we can refuse to be powerless and place our faith in our fight, our battle for our children, our mothers and our fathers, those before us, and those still to come. It is time to

Alice VL

demonstrate how much stronger our faith is, than the evil who works so tirelessly to end us.

It's time to take hands and move onward with integrity and honor, eradicating ourselves of the emotional debt the entitled are so desperate to crucify us with. With our heads down, we free ourselves from the traps placed on our minds and in our hearts. It's time to take each other's hands and step out of the crippling grief of losing our beloved South Africa. A kind of grief we are stuck in and one that has beleaguered us, leaving us in denial. For, we don't understand evil and instead, we become angrier.

Our stories are all different, yet they are all the same. Our grief surges with each attack and each death, while reaching peaks we aren't sure we could emotionally survive. Pretending to quietly cope is sinking us all, one at a time. It's time to take hands and turn the helpless back into the hopeful.

Please take hands …

With love,

Alice VL

Alice VL

A CALL FOR PEACE

I write to ask for change, I am desperate for peace. I am dreaming of the Rainbow Nation that was once promised to all South Africans.

All lives matter. All races count and all of us, each South African dreams of a life of peace, harmony, and unity.

For all the injustices of the past, and for all the injustices of the present, peace can never be achieved through hatred or combining two wrongs to achieve one right.

Peace for a nation that was once built and structured on pride, wealth and beauty.

I dream of a nation in union where all South Africans are home in a country we love, admire, and helped build.

I dream of a Rainbow Nation.

Alice VL

DEAR WORLD

His name is President Cyril Ramaphosa, the ANC elected President of South Africa, and this is what he does, he goes silent, he goes missing. This is how the puppet master rules. In absence and without saying a word to denounce the riots, murders, looting, attacks against the minorities, corruption, crime, money laundering, theft by his cabinet, and the calls to "kill the Boer." He remains silent while his puppets burn anything and everything they can set a match to, even and preferably humans as they continue the tradition of necklacing introduced and left behind by Nelson and Winnie Mandela. His silence is perceived as a secret nod of approval for his puppets to carry on; loot, murder, riot, destroy and leave nothing behind in their path of destruction. Like the coward he is, and has proven over and over again, he cowers away, and hides out until the dust settles, but only until the very next time. While South Africa burns, while 'xenophobic' attacks rummage through our cities, his gangster ally, Ace Magashule steps in and demands that black on black violence should stop. All black people are Africans and should be treated as such. They aren't foreigners. The real foreigners are those with a 'white'ish' skin in South Africa. Still, while Cyril Ramaphosa is silent, Julius Malema urges black South Africans to turn their anger and frustration to the white monopoly.' The *real* foreigners. The *real* thieves. "I think these whites must for a second keep quiet because we are dealing with a mess created by them. Our anger is directed at the wrong people." Andile Mngxitama, leader of BFLF says, "Current looting and riots are a 'dress rehearsal' for the civil war against whites." *Cyril Ramaphosa remains silent.*

Instead, he leaves and solicits investments from outside the borders of South Africa, telling the world that all is well with our country, and our people. He commands that murder statistics against farmers and the targeted minority South Africans are manipulated, mainstream media to be silenced, and he assures you all that there are *no* attacks against the minorities of South Africa, but that crime is simply high. He tells you that land theft (expropriation without compensation) is essentially legal, and will be dealt with in an orderly fashion, yet, what he doesn't tell you is that he will be amending our constitution to legally steal our homes from us. You believe him despite the footage and reports that surface. You all believe *in* him despite the crimes and corruption of his cabinet, even his own questionable activities. You say things like South Africa is a 'resilient democracy' and it is safe for all South Africans, despite your own travel warnings to your citizens.

You all point fingers at us, the so-called racists and white supremacists, yet, Anglo has left. Continental Tyres is out. Whirlpool has taken a financial hit just to be gone. There are more. In total, South Africa has lost 83,000 businesses since 2007.

When is your planned holiday to South Africa? Where is your investment business in South Africa? Instead, you send financial aid just to be done with it. Just so you don't have to deal with it. Just so that the looting, thefts and crimes can continue. In other words, you have done your bit. South Africa has never needed any 'help' before, not even when we were sanctioned. Our ZAR value was of the strongest, even stronger than the USA for a good few years. We have never needed financial aid before, yet, you can't seem to connect the dots, or admit to any of this.

You, the world outside – that's the *you* I am referring to. You, the enablers of a murderous, corrupt warlord and his demonic soldiers. You, who continues giving and essentially, support the current ANC terrorist government. You, who know that the killings are happening, but takes an ANC terrorist's word for it when he says it is nothing more than 'made up internet crimes.'

Alice VL

I hope that it is well with your soul. I hope that you can stand to look at yourself in the mirror, and I hope you can sleep knowing you are enabling instead of condemning or rescuing.

Alice VL

US; FOR YOU, SOUTH AFRICA

South Africa, we stand up and salute you with honour and pride. So many have been stolen from us by your enemy, and those that remain, continue to get up each morning just to lay down our heads each night, under your skies, and under your stars. You serve your countrymen just like you served our fathers before us. You nurture our lands for our sons to cultivate after us. To grow up contented and free just as we did, and just as our ancestors did before us.

We wake up each morning, here where our souls live, just trying to be fathers raising sons, and nurturing daughters. We spend our days offering our everything to you, our home, and we close off our nights, just to do it all over again tomorrow, here where we call our lands home. Bright and early, we begin our days, dressed in old pairs of jeans, scuffed pairs of boots, and old straw hats that the sun beats down on from sunrise to sunset. We don't do it for the wealth or the bills we must pay, for there is no glory in farming our lands, yet we do it anyway.

Alice VL

We work our fields for our sons and for our daughters. We get up each day and work tirelessly on their future. Just as our fathers had once carved out our dreams for us, and just as his father had carved out the same dreams for him.

For your enemies have emptied the streets that once bustled with life. Women in bright dresses have laid down their baskets, and no longer search through windows for fine clothing and little luxuries. The laughter of children playing amongst crowds have become silent, and all we are left with are filthy streets and eerie echoes that wail out in the distance.

The enemy continues to march over fractured sidewalks, leaving empty shells and broken windows on their paths to destruction. The tense hatred as they hurriedly find their next target to scorch, hangs like a dark, sickening stench in the air.

South Africa, as they continue to burn you down, spill our blood in the soil that flows into your rivers and seas, we no longer cry or fear like we used to. We are mourning with you, our beloved home – our beloved South Africa.

Our war isn't about soldiers carrying guns, preparing to meet the enemy on level playing fields. It has come to find us by the color of our skin. It seeks out our mothers, fathers, children

Alice VL

and babies. It seeks to destroy all that is Godly, and all that we call home.

So, while the enemy fights to push you closer to the end; in the soil of your lands, in the heart of our country, we will draw the line. We will hold up our heads, all the way from our farmlands to our towns. We've had to rough it out once or twice before, and while we are faced with the darkest of days, we are going to tough it out once more for you, our sacred home. From our cornfields to our cattle, from our sunflowers to our wheat, we will once again rejoice in our home-country pride. We could never be run out, for our souls wander and roam these lands. This is where our freedom lies. This is where we fall to our knees and look up to the sky. This is where we find our grace. This is where we find our strength. This is where we get up, stronger and braver than before.

From every mountainside and every ocean shore, from the bush to our forests, we will bow our heads once more, fold our hands and close our eyes. Our mountains and our hills, our valleys and our wilderness, our forests and our deserts, our coastlines and grasslands, leave us breathless as it reminds us of what we are struggling for. The best of the entire world is under your sun, and it is what our fathers gave their lives for.

Alice VL

We have faced ferocious thunderstorms and intense rains, but nothing has prepared us for the wickedness of your enemy, our enemy. In the cowardly faces of your rivals, we see the malice in their eyes, we feel the hatred as our African skies turn to darkness. We suffer the shadows in their souls as their hunger for blood and destruction grows stronger. Yet, they have already lost to us, we aren't able to surrender. We have never been taught how to admit defeat as we linger on our knees and cast our eyes upon the heavens of God and of country. For, with every beat of our hearts, our love for you grows stronger, and with every beat of the enemy's heart, their hatred intensifies, yet weakens them. The opponent we face from our knees; a battle we can never lose, a combat that will again, set us free from those who have become our attackers, those who lead armies against your men, and those who are blindly led into robbing us of our freedom, our lands and our lives.

As courage continues to grow and trickle inside of us, we extend to you, our country, our love and our loyalty, our hearts and our souls. The inferno in our breaths as it fills the air with thunder and lightning so that we can lay down the flag the enemy uses to cover up the shame of destroying your people, in your name and as if it's God's will. We lift our arms to our home to

Alice VL

cherish your history, so that some day, we can romance our heritage once again.

For the call to warfare is something the world would never hear us say, instead, we hear the call from our hearts."

Alice VL

HOW DID WE GET HERE?

When I heard about Piet Els' attack a few months ago, I was overcome with absolute dread at the mere thought of such a violent and brutal attack on a name we all knew so well. An attack on a defenseless man of 86.

Piet Els (86), a well-known Kimberley, Northern Cape businessman was buried on his farm, Carters Ridge in May 2018, the same farm where he and Magrietha (Rikkie) Alsemgeest (66) were attacked and tortured by four attackers who forced themselves into their farmhouse during the early morning hours of January that same year.

Piet Els was so severely injured that he was admitted to the Intensive Care Unit but died as a result of his injuries almost four months later.

Both Piet Els and Rikkie were brutally assaulted and burnt with a clothing iron in what was supposed to be the safety of their bedroom and their home. What was more shocking was when reports announced an additional charge of rape that was added to the initial charge of assault. While in the hospital recovering from her injuries, Rikkie said that the attack on them took place between 1 am and 2 am that Wednesday morning in January. They were both asleep when attackers broke down their kitchen door in an attempt to gain entry to the farmhouse. They woke up but dismissed the noise as that of their farm animals.

When four attackers broke through a door that leads to the bedrooms, she at once realized that they were under siege.

The attackers had disconnected their electricity and an emergency generator, leaving them blinded by the dark and especially vulnerable to the armed attackers. Not only were they carrying weapons, but Rikkie noticed that they were carrying what looked like steel rods.

While attacking Piet Els with steel rods, the attackers demanded the location of the safe. When Rikkie told them where the safe was, they ripped off her nightdress, and beat her with the steel rods before they burnt her with a clothing iron on her legs and her head.

They eventually taped her mouth closed and bound her feet while her hands were tied up behind her. While viciously beating Piet Els, they demanded he open the safe, but he couldn't get it open in the dark, and while being so severely assaulted.

Alice VL

The attackers finally tied him up and burnt him with the same clothing iron on his legs and on his back, before they began hitting and kicking him.

When the attackers found a grinder in a shed, they eventually opened the safe and cleared it out before making their getaway in Piet's car almost three hours later.

When Rikkie finally managed to alert emergency services, they found Piet with a fractured skull, burn wounds and extensive injuries all over his body.

How could Piet and Rikkie have known that their turn would come a few short hours after climbing into bed that night? How vulnerable and especially terrifying it must have been to wake up to four armed intruders around their bed, ready to inflict a kind of brutality on them that we cannot even imagine? What was rushing through the mind of an 86-year-old man unable to defend or protect his partner from a vicious assault?

The town of Kimberley was flung into a state of disbelief and utter sadness, which turned into downright despair and broken hearts when he ultimately died a few months later.

I was silent. Around me, the world went silent as we tried to make sense of the cruelty. We just couldn't understand how so much hatred could seep into the lives of two vulnerable people, unable to defend themselves.

As much as I try, I can't make sense of the horrific attack against a man who contributed greatly towards his town and community; the Piet Els who rallied around making Nelson Mandela's first visit to Kimberley an enormous success.

The aftereffects of his murder and the thousands before him will continue to linger and fester within me and a million others for years to come. (1)

It was senseless. They are all meaningless. Just as pointless as the attack against Monty McCormack and his family only two years before.

In 2016, Monty McCormack (73) came back to South Africa for a visit at the smallholding in Rodora, Doornfontein where his son Kennith lived after he had emigrated to the United Kingdom a few years before.

Between the night of the 9th, and the morning of the 10th March, his family in the UK became concerned when their calls to him remained unanswered, and they couldn't reach him. When a family friend in South Africa was asked to check on him, he was horrified to discover Monty's body bludgeoned to death.

Alice VL

Once Monty's body was discovered, they found Marietjie's body lying in a pool of her own blood, beaten to death by what authorities assumed to be with a hammer they found next to her, in a house that Kennith and Marietjie were building.

Only a day later did they find Kenny's body beaten to death with a garden spade, in an orchard of trees on the smallholding when police searched for him with their Air Wing Unit. Other than the family's Mercedes SUV, nothing else was reported stolen.

Pictures from the scene show four slices of toast on a chest freezer in the kitchen. Four slices that were buttered next to an open tub of margarine and an opened tin of apricot jam, not yet spread. Monty and his granddaughter, Kayla, never got the chance to eat them.

What came as deeply disturbing was that Monty's blood was spattered against the wall next to Kayla's bed, with blood smears on her 'Frozen' pillow where he was battered to death with a crowbar.

Another horrific scene was found in the shed when they stumbled upon Kayla's lifeless body, her hands still tied with wire. Blood stains depicting a shoe print on cement bags told the story of a little girl terrified and desperate to get away before being strangled by her attackers.

Kayla was 9 years old. She was defenseless and harmless. She must have been panic-stricken throughout the vicious attack not only on her, but on her grandfather and her parents. What did Kayla see?

How brutal it must have been for her to witness the absolute hatred in the eyes of her attackers.

What does Kayla know about 'turns'? How could she have imagined that her turn would come at the end of just another ordinary day? How many times did she call out for her mommy, and how many of those calls did Marietjie hear while knowing she was powerless to protect her daughter from the brutality of their attackers?

When a memorial service for Kayla was held at the school she attended, her classmates wept as they held each other's hands. A classroom of 9-year-olds faced with the grim reality that they too, might be next. But they didn't quite understand until a counselor at her primary school used a puppet show to explain the concept of death to Kayla's Grade 3 classmates.

The innocence of children lost forever. The trauma of hearing about Kayla's death would linger forever. They will never be the same. Life would never be as it once was for any of them.

(2)

Alice VL

I am a South African. Not an immigrant. Not a settler. Not an illegal, and not a thief. I was born and raised in South Africa, my home. The only home I have ever known. Here, where my footprints can be found below thousands of others when I took my very first steps. Here, where I walked up many paths, down many dirt roads, and through countless streets. Footprints that are buried under a million others just like mine, with a story such as mine.

South Africa is filled with exquisite beaches, beautiful countrysides, and rugged mountain backdrops. My skin has felt the South African sun burn on it, my hair can testify to the South Easterly winds and my hands have dug into the soil of our lands.

Here, my heart fell in love with a rainbow nation of Afrikaners, Xhosas, Zulus, Coloureds, Indians, Khoi-San and many more. Here, I have embraced traditions and the ways of the Boer, which I, an English South African, came to love and adopt.

I remember climbing into bed as a child with an unlocked, often open, front or back door without any fear of harm or danger. I remember my father leaving his car keys in the ignition of his car out in the road. I remember walking to school and riding my bicycle through the streets of the town I was raised in.

What I cannot remember is violence, hatred, poverty, or

Alice VL

murder. The South African Police were feared. The army, navy and air force were respected.

I remember beautiful, clean, equipped, and staffed hospitals. I remember welcoming classrooms, and teachers who taught with passion. I remember values, integrity, honesty, and loyalty. I remember how our love for our country made a family out of strangers.

I wasn't raised according to Apartheid in the Apartheid era. I had never heard the word segregation before. My friends were black, coloured and Indian, and I never knew, or even suspected that they were different from me. I never even noticed.

But, by the time I became a teenager, it was clear that South Africa was changing. There was something in the air that changed when we began hearing words like black, white, racist and apartheid. It was almost as though the South African sky was changing, the air no longer seemed as crisp and fresh as it once was.

There was a shift somewhere. Hatred hung like stale tobacco in the air around us, almost as though a switch between love and hatred had been flipped. By the time I was in my early twenties, Apartheid was abolished, but the beginning of racial tension was felt by all South Africans.

In the years that followed, the murder rate increased, unemployment had crippled citizens, poverty sky-rocketed and children were oddly allowed to engage in sex with each other from as young as twelve-years-old.

It turns out that it wasn't as odd as I thought, it has always been about the numbers. It was about outnumbering white South Africans and turning them into the minority. It was about seizing land from the minority we are accused of stealing.

How naive we were to have believed the call for peace, love, and unity when it was never on the agenda, to begin with. South Africans dreamed of the Rainbow Nation. It is home to millions of us who were born here, raised here, and whose forefathers fought in the Boer wars for the independence and the survival of this country.

But, much of the beauty I was once so proud of has been destroyed. My country is being burnt to the ground and hacked to pieces while my president turns a blind eye to the reality of farm murders.

In early 2018 when it was announced that President Jacob Zuma had stepped down and that Cyril Ramaphosa would succeed him, there was a glimmer of hope that the shift we were hoping for, would finally end the chaos and lawlessness in South Africa.

But, all hope for a better, safer South Africa was crushed just days after President Cyril Ramaphosa addressed the nation in his first official broadcasted speech. He announced that Boer land, white South African land will be expropriated without compensation, and without delay. (3)(4)(5) White land *only*. Our land. Our traded for or paid for land. Land which had been in families for hundreds of years.

The murder rate amongst farmers and white South Africans suddenly makes sense. The list of names of murdered South Africans grows longer, the same murders my president denies, or my government re-classifies as normal crimes.

I scroll down, and as I take in each of the names before me, I realize that this list only guarantees one thing; there will be thousands more. (6)

I don't want to admit it too loudly, but I know, and others like me *know*, there is a slow erupting, but progressive war that is playing out against white South Africans, and it has been going on for years.

Alice VL

Is seizing white-owned land perhaps hiding a darker agenda? I can't ignore or dismiss the anger and hatred directed at white South Africans. I can't hide the fact that the color of my skin is a crime in the very country I was born in.

We try to keep ourselves, our children, and our homes safe, but we fail. Each time there is an invasion, we have failed despite the measures we have taken. We try and support our families with the bare minimum. Our men who are unemployable because they are too white, resort to odd jobs here and there, at all and any hour of the day or night, simply to put food on the table.

At night, after we have locked ourselves away from the world, we listen for unusual and unfamiliar noises and sounds. Each night, I know it could be my turn, and that of my family's. What I don't know is how many attackers will surround my bed before I wake up. I lay in bed as the hours tick by, and I *wait*. I don't want to be awoken by armed men ready to inflict brutality on my children, or me. As I try and calm my greatest fears, I listen for unfamiliar sounds. My heart pounds a mile a minute with each new, unidentified sound.

Most nights, I don't sleep. Nobody sleeps. Most nights, I lay awake and think of a neighbor, perhaps a family member that was attacked only days before.

How my world has changed. I don't drive at night, and we no longer sit in our gardens, day or night. How terrifying the shadows have become as they walk by my home. How unnerving the voices in the distance are.

I listen to others around me, they don't say much, but the fear in their eyes reminds me that we are all just waiting for our turn. I live from day to day praying that my turn, and that of those I love would skip us.

I know that when they do come for my family and me, we won't stand a chance against the fight that will come in like a thief in the night. The numbers will infiltrate my home, my safe place, when they come for us.

My heart is broken. My footprints are covered in the blood of people like me. I feed off the soil where blood is spilled, every single day. It flows through our lands, into our rivers and dams, and hangs like a foggy mist in the air.

White South Africans are slowly being stripped of our Afrikaner pride, making us vulnerable, and weakening us all at the same time.

I hear the songs loudly sung around me; 'Kill The Boer,'

Alice VL

and it comes back to haunt me in the darkest hours of the night.
(7)(8)(9)(10)(11)(12)(13)(14)(15)(16)(17)(18)(19)(20)(21)(22)

I hear them loudly call for our children to be slaughtered and used as fertilizer in the same lands that feed us all. (23) My country is divided, and I am being forced to distinguish between color—something I, and most white South Africans have never had to do before.

My race is thrown at me and used against me almost every day. I am branded a thief and a racist simply because of the color of my skin. I am punished. I am persecuted. I am hated. I am a criminal because I am white.

My country victimizes me, my family and other South Africans, simply because we wear a coat in the wrong color. I can't seek employment; my government won't allow me to. My president won't allow my children to carve out a future for themselves. My president doesn't care if tonight is perhaps, *my turn*.

Tomorrow morning, he won't even know my name. My life does not matter to my president, or to my country.

Tomorrow morning, he will tell the world once more that there are *no* farm murders in South Africa, and my death, or that of my children, will be classified as normal crime.

Alice VL

MY TURN – SOUTH AFRICA

Because, I am white, my turn will come.

I live through each hour, minute and second of each day with a target on my back. I listen with sadness when I'm told I am not human or worthy, because I am white. There aren't laws that are enforced to protect me, or those like me in South Africa. The ANC law is molded and shaped to work against me. *It isn't fair.*

I am no-one. I am not one of great importance. I am as insignificant as the next white South African. I am just one of the thousands facing genocide by a criminal and corrupt government which not only includes our number one employee, President Cyril Ramaphosa, but his entire cabinet.

I am no-one. I am just another South African that is crippled by fear, debilitated by unemployment, and I am losing the heritage I adopted as a child. I am one whose blood will eventually be spilled in the same soil where thousands of others have been spattered in.

But, as I prepare to surrender to my bleak reality, I hear that Australia acknowledges our position. I see that New Zealand, Russia and a certain few South African expats in Britain are finally recognizing the brutal and horrendous attacks against white South Africans. I am afraid to hope, but I do anyway. So do most South Africans desperate to hold onto hope. (24)(25)(26)

Alice VL

They all agree, the numbers are incontestable, and the message is clear; brutal and gruesome attacks against farmers are being launched in an attempt to claim dictatorship over South Africa. Minister Peter Dutton sparked enormous controversy earlier in 2018 when he said, 'I think these people deserve special attention and we're certainly applying that special attention now.' (27)

And then, as expected, his statement led to a diplomatic spat between Australia and South Africa. Our International Relations Minister Lindiwe Sisulu later issued a diplomatic demarche, or course of action to the Australian High Commissioner in South Africa, Adam McCarthy, and demanded that Minister Dutton retract his comments at once, disparaging the claims by the minority South Africans. (28)

So was UK Independence Party member Janice Atkinson condemned after she wrote to the British Foreign Secretary Boris Johnson, imploring him to step in and prevent South Africa from becoming 'another Zimbabwe.' (29)

Subsequently, Russia has recently accepted a number of Boer farmers from South Africa. 'It's a matter of life and death—there are attacks on us. It's got to the point where the politicians are stirring up a wave of violence. The climate here [Stavropol

Region] is temperate, and this land is created by God for farming. All this is very attractive.' A South African farmer was quoted as saying shortly after his arrival. (30)

Here is anger and here is hatred. A kind of abhorrence that rears its ugly head during farm attacks and home invasions. Attacks that are protracted and drawn-out until the very end so that torment and suffering can be effectively applied.

I shudder at the practices of torture which includes the burning of victims, forcing boiling water into them and over them, compelling them to drink chemicals such as bleach, sodomizing them with foreign objects, raping and torturing their wives, daughters, and mothers and then finally, beating, stabbing, or shooting them to death.

I am overwhelmed, devastated and heartbroken when I hear of children that are strangled, drowned in boiling water, or that their heads are crushed with objects, or smashed against walls. I can barely imagine the thoughts that rush through the minds of the men who are forced to watch the brutality inflicted upon those they love, as they helplessly sit by and see their wives or children die before they too, are tortured and killed. The message remains clear; *kill the Boer—kill the farmer.*

I hear from farmers who have survived attacks. They are

Alice VL

adamant that these assaults were done in revenge or carried out as hate crimes. Some say that they were politically motivated or encouraged by the powers that be.

Again, I don't want to admit the fact that there have been too many attacks and too many murders to shrug off and justify as *normal* crimes, or crimes of opportunity.

The public hatred being spewed towards us, the minority South Africans. The threats, the demands, and the warnings leave me with little to no doubt, that we are vulnerable targets, and that our *turn* is coming. My turn to be exposed to these heinous crimes is only a matter of time. Each day, I wonder whether today will be my turn, and if not mine, who's?

I am taken aback when I hear other countries say, 'We had no idea—none of this reaches us.' I lower my head, and I understand once again that there are filters in place to sieve out the true state of the inhumane gruesomeness taking place against farmers and white South Africans.

I am frustrated by the reality that the horror and torture applied during these murders are not reported in mainstream media. The statistics given by my government and the numbers given by private organizations, don't correspond.

Alice VL

I am sad that my government downplays the truth about these murders as they keep the numbers low by classifying these extraordinary crimes as ordinary.

Perhaps, there still is a chance that our children can grow up without the fear of losing their parents in an attack during the night. Perhaps they too can survive and grow up in a world where their lives matter. Perhaps, my president will realize that a twelve-year-old child who is allowed consensual sex with another child of fourteen or sixteen is *still* only a child. These are still children. Yet, the law says they're not—not really. Or, is this how the war is waged on me, my family and all white South Africans? (31)

What about the Economic Freedom Fighters, or Black First Land First, who have openly called for the persecution of white South Africans by means of chanting 'struggle-songs' which was shown to encourage, and inspire farm murders?

But, what happens when there is a glimpse from outsiders into the true state of South Africa?

I was stunned when I heard that Lauren Southern and Katie Hopkins, both international independent journalists, recently paid a visit to South Africa to investigate, and ultimately reported on South Africa's farm attacks and killings. I held my breath when Katie Hopkins' reporting on the 'dreadful situation that continues in South Africa' saw her being detained at the OR Tambo International Airport. Would her detention silence her? (32)

Since their trip to South Africa, Lauren Southern released a documentary titled, 'Farmlands' in which she depicts the seriousness of the genocidal situation in South Africa. At last, the world would hear the truth about what we are afraid to say out loud. (33)

Still, when farmer Willem Roux had his eyes pulled out by a pair of pliers by his attackers, the South African Police was quoted as referring to farm attacks as "house or ordinary robbery." (34)

Again, I realize how the numbers are collected and how these attacks are classified as 'minor crimes' by the South African Police Service. Our government says its *minor* crimes. My president is downplaying the seriousness of these attacks in South Africa, as he blatantly manipulates the statistics to South Africans, and to the rest of the world. Are the whispers true? Is this the evidence everyone is talking about? Is our president covering up the fact that these killings are orchestrated?

I am reminded of the more than six hundred police case-dockets that have disappeared from police stations during a five-year period, and I realize again how widespread the corruption is right here in South Africa. (35)

Hopelessness sets in as the criminal justice system continues to fail us while creating an environment in which crime continues to escalate and flourish. This means that attacks increase because it is 'okay'—the attackers see it as been given the green light. But, it also means that the victims of these crimes, us, the vulnerable, are becoming increasingly bitter and angry towards not only the 'sides' launching these attacks, but towards our president.

Anger and rage is increasing by the day as our government not only fails to, but refuses to protect the most vulnerable. We just can no longer ignore the fact that crimes against us appears to be endorsed.

I hear President Ramaphosa tell the world that there are no farm attacks or murders in South Africa, and that there are no land grabs taking place. I am stunned, and then I realize why these crimes are continuing and increasing in violence; my president refuses to acknowledge that we are a tribe, *dying*.

My president is covering up the true state of murders in South Africa, and in turn, those seeking to destroy us are protected by him and his government. Not once has my president stood up, and committed to protecting us, the minority in South Africa from the slaughter against us.

Not once has my president reassured any of us that the law applies to us all, and that we will be protected as South Africans. Instead, we watch daily as our corrupt parliament, government officials, cabinet and presidents are protected under their laws.

Only if I were to fight in a different color and in the name of 'struggle' and 'oppression,' will I be protected under the South African Law.

Where does that leave me, my family, and the remainder of the white South African population? Vulnerable. Oppressed. Disadvantaged. Segregated. Intimidated. Dying.

Isn't this apartheid all over again?

We are trapped in a volatile country filled with racial tension, intense loathing, fear, and notable division while protests escalate into violent rioting, looting and burning almost on a daily basis.

We live in fear as we are constantly being threatened that our lands and our lives will be taken. My president remains

Alice VL

silent while the Economic Freedom Fighters and Black First Land First continues to deliberately mislead their 'people' with fabricated statistics and thwarted history lessons in an attempt to create a frenzy while undoubtedly scoring political points.

My president remains silent when blood continues to spill from white South Africans and flows into the farmlands, he is so desperate to seize. I hear whispers about genocide, and I listen to some talk about ethnic cleansing. I consider farmers who have survived attacks, adamant that their attackers have had some form of military training.

They are convinced that the attacks on them are planned by our government in an attempt to intimidate them and drive them from their lands by subjecting them to inhumane physical trauma and heinous acts like the torturing of a loved one.

We live in chaos. We are regularly faced with protests that take place in towns or on our highways, all of which eventually turn violent. The South African Police keep at a distance, almost as though they are afraid to enforce the law. Or, is there simply no desire to enforce the law? By the striking number of criminal records against a number of police officers, I must wonder whether they are at all willing to enforce the law.

I hear about my neighbors, family members, and friends

who have reached their turn. I become angry, desolate and I am heartbroken, but only for a moment. For a moment, I sit down and recall the horror they must have suffered. I reflect for a moment longer, and then I get up, and get on with the life I am being forced to lead. We can't wallow too long. We must go on.

I listen to the contradictions of the world, and pray that somewhere, someone sees the turmoil around us. I know that our cries for help are being criticized by the outside world.

At this very moment, someone somewhere in South Africa is fighting for his life, and that of his family. Somewhere out there a child is screaming because his mother is being raped, and his father is being tortured. In the dark of the night, the boogeyman has come home to a little boy or a little girl and is slaughtering his parents before that monster will ultimately, butcher him.

The screams ring out in the deadness of the night, but nobody hears. Nobody sees. Tomorrow morning when the world wakes up, they will find this family in a pool of their own blood.

Tortured. Beaten. Killed.

They will find a father who fought back with his last breath. They will find a mother who was desperate to protect her child, and they will find a child whose eyes had to witness how cruelly and heartlessly his parents were tormented.

They will look at their lifeless bodies and will barely be able to imagine what had taken place only a few hours before. They will stare into their unresponsive eyes and wonder what the last thing was any one of them saw. Their blood will flow just like thousands before them.

They will become a number and falsified statistic, before a white cross is erected for them on a privately-owned farmland somewhere in South Africa. Their names will be added to the list, and they will be forgotten a few hours later when the next murder takes place.

Soon, I may no longer see these lists or count the crosses.

Tonight, it might be my turn, it might be my child's turn.

Alice VL

MY TURN – SOUTH AFRICA

Alice VL

VIVA KILL THE BOER – KILL THE FARMER 1993

In 1990, when Nelson Mandela was released from prison, the fear leading up to his release had disappeared within moments of listening to him address the South AFrican nation.

His words echoed throughout South Africa when he announced that there will be no more hatred. There will be no more warfare. There will be no more segregation, and there will be no revenge. He spoke of his dream in which he envisioned a country in unity. He spoke of the Rainbow Nation.

When an ANC drafted circular appeared on social media a few years ago, it suddenly dawned on us that the Rainbow Nation and calls for unity was nothing more than a smokescreen. How could we even begin to fathom that a slow war was planned and executed as far back as 1993 against white South Africans? *Against us.*

It made way for a new kind of fear, a new kind of hopelessness, and brand-new sentiments of defeat. *We never saw it coming.*

Alice VL

CIRCULAR 213-6
AFRICAN NATIONAL CONGRESS
JUNE 1993
THE SUCCESS STORY: OUR STRUGGLE FOR LIBERATION

1.   The armed and constant threat of violence forced the

white, spineless regime to negotiate for so-called peace.

2.   The psychological warfare through the churches to create a guilt complex with whites was a victory over Christians.

3.   The MASS ACTION was a successful method to rip the national economy to pieces and create panic in the rich settlers.

4.   The constant uproar in Black Education is the fourth try for liberation through education because the white regime simply cannot meet all our demands.

5.   All four tactical attacks leave the regime powerless and gradually giving in to our demands.

6.   All these help to create a feeling of helplessness and despair and to lose confidence in their government.

Be careful not to upset the farmers too much before we gain control over the SAP (South African Police Service) and SADF

Alice VL

(South African National Defence Force).

7. The constant pressure of violence and economic uncertainty force De Klerk to surrender power to the suppressed people like in Namibia.

AFFIRMATIVE ACTION STRATEGY AFTER APRIL 27, 1994

The greatest fear of the white settler is to lose his job, his farm or his house and all the luxuries! This will enable the new DEMOCRATIC GOVERNMENT to tax them to the utmost while our comrades in MK and APLA continue with their part of the struggle.

1. Surplus land will be redistributed among our people.

2. All positions in public service will be replaced by comrades.

3. The security forces will be reconstructed with our comrades to protect our people. Whites were protected

for

350 years. Get them experience to be second class citizens!

4. No ammunition will be available to white settlers.

5. Health institutions will be Africanised, and whites will pay according to their income to enable thus to

contribute

Alice VL

to their liberated brothers.

6.   Some white schools will be allowed because most settlers

> will pay their last cent for white education and this will provide some money for our people.

8.   Pension funds and insurance companies collected billions over the years, will be at our disposal for education of our comrades in years to come.

VIVA KILL A BOER KILL A FARMER

Viva. Kill the Boer, kill the farmer. In other words, rejoice. (36)(37)(38)

Not once has the ANC government refuted Circular 213-6 or the validity thereof. Yet, when we consider each clause of this document, we realize how accurately it reflects the current situation in South Africa.

We are branded as settlers and thieves. Our lives don't matter, and it seems, never did. I feel betrayed, just like my neighbors, friends, and family feel betrayed. We feel threatened, hated and worthless.

My government has succeeded in weakening us through promises of a Rainbow Nation and equality. We were gullible. We were hopeful of a Rainbow Nation.

Alice VL

It crept up on us. The hatred. The job market exclusion. Land redistribution. When white public service employees were offered attractive retrenchment packages, we never once considered the fact that it was simply an effort to economically empower black South Africans while crippling the rest of us, all at the same time.

Education was immediately downgraded throughout South African schools. Health institutions suffered tremendously when staff employed were ill-equipped for nursing positions.

We never saw it coming. We thought we were building South Africa together. We thought that we all had one ideal in mind; to make South Africa great. We thought that we, the black, white, colored and the Indian communities were functioning well together.

And then, the reality dawned on me when Cyril Ramaphosa was inaugurated as president of South Africa; he was a senior member of the ANC at the time Circular 213-6 was circulated. (39)

Cyril Ramaphosa was respected for the positions he's held in the past. A much-needed leader we thought would lift South Africa from the chaos we were drowning in as successfully as he managed his multi-million-dollar companies.

Alice VL

But, he turned a blind eye to the degeneration of our schools, the collapse of health services, and the crippling of health schemes. He turned a blind eye to the murders of white farmers, and in the process, he turned white South Africans into second-class citizens.

Was land expropriation and redistribution without compensation part of a twenty-five-year-old strategy as stated in Circular 213-6?

Does it simply re-iterate what we already know; that the ANC has never surrendered their feuds against white South Africans?

This document tells me in no uncertain terms that black South Africans have never declared peace, and never *intended* to live in harmony with any other race, but their own. There was a Rainbow Nation. The dream of a Rainbow Nation was never real. They, the majority have simply altered their tactics, and turned my South Africa into a slow-brewing combat, about to erupt in civil war.

Has my president engaged in a slow-war-tactic in an effort to keep it veiled from the rest of the world as my government methodically rids South Africa of the white population, thereby, ethnically cleansing the country?

Alice VL

Why does my president disregard the attacks against our whites? Or does his ignorance support the fact that our court system in place is programmed to execute ANC policy and not the South African law?

My president refuses to hear us. My government won't listen to our cries for help. Instead, the ANC government brands us white supremacists, seeking nothing more than to divide our nation

What do we do? What can we do? *Nothing*. Instead, I get up each morning, and anxiously await the news of the latest attack. By the time I sit down for breakfast with my family, I am silent. My family is edgy. Our hearts are heavy, and my morning coffee leaves me with a bitter taste in my mouth. It is eerily quiet as we push our breakfast to the side. The smell of murder hangs in the air.

We smile at one another as we desperately try not to surrender to our fears. We appear brave, but we're terrified. When the numbness starts setting in, we get up from the breakfast table, and we carry on living as normally as possible.

We can't win even though we are disqualified from universities through restrictive quota enrollment programs. We are barred from sports teams through enforced quota systems, and we are excluded from the right to life through targeted hate crimes.

We are barred from farming through targeted farm attacks, we are barred from owning land through land expropriation (40), and we are barred from the constitution of equal rights before the law through South Africa's double standards and race-based laws. (41)

We are barred from protection and are continuously exposed to intimidation through songs like 'one settler one bullet' or 'kill the farmer, kill the Boer,' chanted brazenly by political leaders.

Tonight, might be my turn. South Africa waits to see whose turn it will be.

Alice VL

THE MOST DANGEROUS JOB IN THE WORLD

A Farmer's Story

The Northern Cape, South Africa. My farm, my home and the only kind of life we know. I am a farmer's wife. A proud one. I get to share the land with a man that was born on these very grounds sixty years ago; the middle child of three children. His grandfather and father farmed this land until December 1989 when we took over the reins, and with both hands, we clutched firmly onto the opportunity to continue our family legacy, farming in South Africa.

It was never an easy life. It was not without challenges and hardships, but it was worth it. These lands flow like blood through our veins and are filled with decades of love formed with a million stories carried down from generation to generation. It is our home and emotions flow equally through our bloodstream.

Our home; the home my farmer brought me to, to begin our lives together is nestled against a road used by the public on a daily basis, but, it is quiet. Traffic is light, and passersby are few.

Alice VL

Our closest neighbors are at least a mile away, but a little country café is right next to us. We must be about ten families that live relatively close to each other, yet three of these families have chosen to live in town and only 'visit' their farms over weekends.

I remember the day my farmer brought me here to my home for the very first time. We were exposed. Our home and lands were testaments to the calmness and freedom of peace, quiet and security. There was no fencing, no brick walls around our home; there were no security measures in place. It wasn't necessary. There just was no crime.

When I reflect back to those years, the worst possible mishap that could affect any farmer was if one head of livestock was perhaps stolen and slaughtered. How different that reality is today. The hoofs of our livestock are sliced and chopped as they allow them to suffer. The cruelty. The reality.

We quickly found our way around our farmlands and dug in with our hearts and our souls as we offered to the land our blood, sweat, and tears. We raised children, and we welcomed grandchildren to the same lands my farmer's parents did before him.

But, in 1994, everything changed when the ANC

government was elected. Farm murders began almost from that very moment. So tragic.

Farmers are murdered. Brutally. Cruelly. Heartlessly. Thousands. We became apathetic. We barely realized it, but when we did, we understood why. We had to. We had to survive. So, we closed our eyes, we prayed, we believed, and we had faith, but we carried on. We became harder, there was no other option. There was no other alternative.

When ex-President FW De Klerk's first wife, Marijke was murdered in her home in the Cape, even though it was not a farm murder, it shocked us. It shocked the entire country. After all, she lived in a security complex.

Murder is one thing, but the brutality and cruelty is something the entire farming community will never be able to accept as normal. It can never be understood, and it can never be something we will ever get used to.

Daily, we are forced to face the torture involved in these attacks; boiling water, broken bones and broken knees, rape, setting victims alight, panga attacks, slitting of throats, fingernails that are torn out, children as young as two years old that are tortured, maimed and raped and so much more.

Alice VL

The farming community throughout South Africa was at once quickly forced to implement measures for our own safety. In 1996, my aunt and I were alone on our farm when a black man showed up carrying papers as evidence that our home was his. Through a window from my home, I tried reasoning with him. I implored him to make an appointment with the Land Claims Commissioner to discuss his claims. This led to sudden and immediate aggression when he demanded I leave my home.

During those early years, mobile phones were not yet available, yet today, landlines are no longer available due to the brazen thefts of copper cables which are stolen quicker than our telecoms company can replace them.

Nevertheless, I placed a frantic call to the South African Police Service and explained the threat outside my home; secured by nothing more than a door. I was shocked when an on-duty policeman responded by advising me that there was, unfortunately, no transportation available to send an officer out to me.

Well, of course, I informed the same officer that should this intended 'land-grabber' make any attempt to enter my home, I would arm myself adequately in an effort to defend two women alone on a farm. Within twenty minutes, the South

African Police Service arrived and showed up on my doorstep. We then realized that our safety was up to us and that we had to regroup and adjust at once.

When land expropriation began back in 1999 in Zimbabwe, we held our breaths. A beautiful country and a food basket of Africa was brought to its knees almost overnight. There was no longer food; poverty reigned, and although money was available, there was nothing anyone could do with it.

Zimbabwean citizens flocked to South Africa seeking food and a better life. Who could blame them? Who could fault them in their desperation? But, we told ourselves and each other that it would never happen here to the farming community in South Africa. How wrong we were. How ignorant we were to the reality that we were being murdered one by one and day by day.

It was only in the years following social media that the truth and realities opened our eyes to the on-going attacks against farmers. Farm murders barely reached newspapers and received little to no attention. However, in this day and age, we are faced with a certain caliber of journalists who fiercely attempt to sway the citizens of South Africa and the world outside that the farm murders are nothing more than a myth.

In the meantime, criminals enter and take anything they

Alice VL

can get their hands on; not only in the suburbs but in the farming community. They come for anything from cables, diesel, and steel, to tools, livestock, and implements. Another home on our farmlands approximately 5km's away has been broken down where windows, doors, frames, roofing, and flooring was stolen until only the remains of what would seem like an old, dilapidated building were left behind.

It is too costly to employ security services to guard our homes. Our farmers work no less than twelve hours each day under the ruthless African sun; how are they supposed to guard our homes at night? What do we do? We look the other way as they continue to destroy these homes and walk away leaving a path of destruction behind them. How tragic? We aim to build. They aim to break down.

At the South African Agricultural Trade Show known as Nampo, you will find a wall of commemoration that lists the names of each and every murdered South African Farmer. I stood in front of that wall, and I sobbed at the numbers before me. I wept for my fellow farmers, and I wept for the brutality of these murders. I wept knowing that we are alone, and I wept at the knowledge that our government is failing to protect us. I wept for my farmlands, and I wept for my people and my country.

Alice VL

Again, we adapt to our circumstances and become numb just to survive in South Africa. It isn't easy but throwing in the towel was never an option. This is our land. This is our heritage. This is where our souls live.

Again, I re-think our role in this, if ever we personally played a part in these kinds of attacks. I am committed to our farm employees, and from the very start, we have worked hard to form solid relationships with each worker who walks onto our farmlands, in need of a job, and with just a suitcase in his hand.

We are kind. We are respectful and show empathy and compassion to each living person that crosses through into our lives. And then, out of the blue, two of our beloved guard dogs die suddenly, not even a month apart. First to die was our four-legged Dolf, a boerboel. Cat flu was diagnosed and, while we are mourning his passing, our second fur child dies. Again, it was attributed to cat flu. Poison was not at all suspected.

In January 2017, while we were going about our daily lives one evening, a phone call comes through from a woman claiming to be a member of the Safety Police informing us that five policemen in an unmarked vehicle were on their way to our farm. She was adamant that we open our farm gate and allow them entry.

Alice VL

My farmer speculated that it might be related to a cow that was slaughtered by an intruder a week earlier. But I knew better. I knew that the sense of urgency and the time of night had nothing to do with a slaughtered cow.

Much to my horror and disgust, they presented us with a 'blueprint to murder.' An informant came forward with a blueprint of an intended attack; one in which a planned farm invasion was imminent on our lands. In our home. Against me. Against my farmer. Against my children. They knew the color of our home. They knew the exact number of occupants in the house at night. They knew that my farmer drove a white Landcruiser. They knew where the keys to his cruiser were kept. And then, the most horrific revelation of all, which sent shivers down my spine; the plan was to torture us, but the attackers were not to leave without the cruiser.

As though I had been lifted from my body, I looked at the scene around me. It felt like I was watching a fast-paced, high-octane movie. It just couldn't be real. How did they know these things? How were they able to accurately point out details such as those stated on the 'blueprint to murder'? Who else knew these things but those we employ? Could it be that those we would hand our last pennies to were behind this?

Alice VL

I can honestly say that I lost faith that day. and that I no longer trusted anyone. ANYONE. How cruel is that? The following morning, four would-be attackers were arrested in two small towns a few miles away. When investigated, it was discovered that all four of these would-be attackers had spent time in prison for murder, armed robbery, and theft, amongst other things. Two are from a town I have never even heard of.

Again, we step up our game and adapt. We go through our fencing with a fine-tooth comb. We install optic fiber cables right around our fencing. We adopt two more guard dogs, and we keep our little ones indoors. We install surveillance cameras right around our home. We install an IP Dome camera that can 'patrol' our home and record any movements around the house and the fencing. We add a further five cameras to the roads around us for the entire community's safety and each car passing through in any direction is captured on camera. Yet, we're not naïve; we know they can come on foot through the fields.

In March 2017, my farmer's defenseless uncle, Piet Jacobs, aged 79, was murdered not more than 50 km's away from our farm. We are still recovering. We are still recuperating. We are still in shock. Sometimes, we still can't believe that it happened. They strangled him. What I can never discard from my mind is the thought that his murderer was the last face he saw.

Alice VL

Through all this, we try to do our best to survive and live 'normally' on our farm. Each day, we complete our daily tasks, sometimes in advance, because we just don't know if tonight might be our turn.

To be a farmer in South Africa is undisputedly one of the most dangerous jobs in the world. There is something so sick, cruel and evil about that. We live a simple life, close to nature and with love for our animals and people. We live close to the earth, and because of that, we are a target. Each day, each hour, and each minute. Can you imagine the fear of our children knowing their parents are vulnerable in their own homes?

On Valentine's Day, 14th February 2018, another one of our community farmers was attacked. 8 km's from us. The attackers heartlessly assaulted a farmer and his wife before they smashed his skull in with an ax. After being admitted to the hospital, the farmer's wife recovered, but the farmer passed away. He was 82 years old.

I beg you! Tell me! Who attacks defenseless old people in their homes? Who can commit such acts of violence with such rage and hatred? Who?

Since then, we have completed weapons training courses; after all, we are fighting a war. Our farms have been turned into war zones. For each moment of each day, we are armed. We owe it to ourselves that we at least have a fighting chance to defend ourselves and our families.

At night, when the world switches off for the night, as we read our Bible, our bullets lay nearby. Before each day begins, I draw my Bible just a little closer, and I pray; it was not our turn yet. I thank God that it was not our turn yet. As soon as I open my eyes to the world again, I wait to hear who's turn it was.

How sad that a Bible and bullets go hand in hand? How unnecessary and senseless the fighting is. How life is no longer, life. At night, our gates are locked, doors are firmly bolted shut, alarm systems are activated, and cameras are checked.

We tend to our pets which include our guard dogs, and the house curtains are closed tightly before we lock ourselves away behind another reinforced security gate that cordoned off our bedrooms from the rest of the house. All bedroom doors are locked and shut off from the others. That is when floodlights are switched on around the house, and our guard dogs are able to patrol effectively.

Then when the darkest of the night is about to be upon us, our Bible is close by, and our prayers are said. Our weapons are loaded and are a permanent fixture on pedestals, on both

Alice VL

sides of our bed. My heart hurts so badly when my young son sends me daily reminders; 'Mom, be safe, please.'

Land expropriation without compensation is a reality for all of us. Farm murders escalate by the day. Employment issues become progressively worse. So, do we choose another life and another way? No. We are Christians. We are hardworking, and honest South Africans. Good must triumph over evil. IT MUST!

Is it easy to stay here on our farmlands and in South Africa? No. It is hell. But, how do you demand that a farmer, especially my farmer, ignore the passion of a Boer and ask him to reject his heritage? How can he when it lives in his heart, in his soul, and in his genes?

Alice VL

THE REALITY OF FARM MURDERS

The cruel reality in South Africa is one where the leaders of our nation are currently embarking on a number of campaigns to discredit and criticize white genocide claims made by us, the minority South Africans. They have nonchalantly labeled it as nothing more than white-driven-propaganda or white supremacy as they continue to control mainstream media's unfair reporting.

Being a farmer in South Africa has become the most treacherous job in the country. What the rest of the world doesn't know is that the already-armed farmer rushes home before the sun sets. His wife back home is waiting for him, and she too is armed and in fear. His son at the other end of the farm is frantic to round up the cattle before he too, rushes home, armed and in fear.

The darkness has become their worst enemy, and the moment the sun sets, they are extraordinarily vulnerable. They no longer have the right to function normally or sleep without fear. They no longer have the right to the safety of their homes and farms where they work to provide for their families, and the families of their workers without fear. They can no longer guarantee shelter.

They are forced to listen to struggle songs like 'Kill The Boer—Kill The Farmer' or to chantings like 'One Settler—One Bullet.' They fear driving out in their fields at night, and they fear sitting in their garden after dark, as they unwind after a long day.

They know they are being brutally attacked and murdered for their land, and it's not a fair fight. Heavily armed attackers come in at night while they are asleep, and bring the numbers with them, determined to rape, torture and kill.

The farmer doesn't say much. If he does, he is accused of causing panic. He works his fields and at the same time, he wonders what the farm murder casualty numbers must be before the world sits up and takes notice. How many more murders will justify panic?

Just the day before, his wife was exposed to a social media call for white 'pigs' to be slaughtered, and have their offspring used as fertilizer.

There are white crosses erected as a memorial for slaughtered farmers. They know their names. They knew them once. They remain quiet, and they remain hopeless and helpless.

Alice VL

If they so much as speak of the atrocities against farmers, they are accused of embellishing the truth even though they can't sleep at night, and even though they have taken every safety precaution that is available to them.

Each door and each window is firmly secured and checked each night. On the dining room table, he keeps his Bible and bullets closeby, as they prepare themselves for the night ahead.

Some of them don't sleep at all, and some take turns keeping vigil and monitoring security systems for outdoor movement. Others simply can't sleep. Every noise, each sound, and every movement is demoralizing. Their lives have been adapted to listen for echoes and thuds that they aren't familiar with. They are afraid, terrified of the numbers that could appear in the darkest of the night.

Their lives are no longer their own. Their decisions now include their defenselessness. They have been stripped of their ability to live and work in safety. They are afraid to seek help. They are afraid of being accused of racism. They know exactly what the consequences are should they seek awareness from the world.

The world is blissfully unaware of the reality that white men, women, and children are being specifical ly targeted for rape, torture, and murder in large numbers and daily.

We *know* we are a mark. We know without a doubt that there might as well be a contract out on all our lives. How can it not be? How do we justify the outrage, hatred, attacks, and murders against white South Africans, perpetrated by black South Africans?

I watch daily, and I mourn daily as white South African farmers experience a full-blown spate of murder and destruction, and for no other reason than our race.

I scroll past, and then I scroll back when I read reports of their houses being vandalized with phrases such as 'Kill the Boer' or 'We're coming for you, Whitey.'

Will the deliberate killings of the white population in South Africa be recognized as an act of genocide only when the last South African Boer or Afrikaner has fallen?

Again, I search in mainstream media, and I fail to find one single report on this. Fake news? Fake reporting on genocide? Over-exaggeration on the true state of South Africa? White supremacy?

All this while we are still reeling from the news that Jacob Zuma and his comrades sourced London-based public relations firm, Bell Pottinger, to drum up anti-white sentiment throughout the world. The investigation into Bell Pottinger's campaign revealed a media empire that included mainstream news outlets, alternative news websites, and a large number of social media platforms which included Twitter, Facebook, and Instagram where large-scale fake news propaganda was launched and as a result, negatively influenced all South Africans.

When the campaign was first exposed, it increased distrust in our government and became clear that the ANC government will go to any lengths to protect themselves and ultimately, ensure that white South Africans become increasingly vulnerable. (42)

The campaign driven between July 2016 and July 2017 was responsible for at least 220,000 fake tweets and Facebook posts to deliberately confuse the world. (43)(44) In July 2017, Bell Pottinger Chief Executive and major shareholder James Henderson resigned after issuing an 'unequivocal' apology for the fake campaign.

An apology. That's it and so, life carries on.

Bell Pottinger's role in configuring the Gupta family's empire was established to veil their increasing enrichment at the expense of South African citizens and taxpayers. But for the fact that a selected group of campaigners who have enjoyed limited access to such reporting on social media, we would never know. Just like you. Just like the rest of the world.

Fake news? Is it fake news when Julius Malema and his allies incite violence by spewing out anti-white sentiment at each and every rally or gathering, he is the 'star' of?

Through all the farm murders and the killing of white South Africans, we are faced with a president who remains pro-active in defending these claims, and in the end, he simply criticizes the word 'genocide.'

A president quick to condemn the entire world, while disrespecting and insulting foreign leaders. Party leaders like Julius Malema who taunts presidents of foreign countries by issuing them with stern warnings to retreat while assuring the rest of the world that they, the leaders of South Africa are not afraid. (45)

Words like 'there will be blood' or 'we are taking back the land' are spewed out on an almost daily basis. When I came across Genocide Watch, an international human rights organization who is specifically concerned with acts of genocide, and rates various countries with strong ethnic or religious conflicts according to ten stages of genocide, I found that South

Africa was rated as being on the border of polarization and preparation which is currently stages 6 and 7. (46) But, that just doesn't seem accurate anymore. Stage 8 is defined as persecution, and stage 9 advances to genocide. And there it was, stage 10 - the denial of genocide.

Denial.

Genocide Watch is justifiably disturbed with the high murder rates in South Africa, specifically the unbalanced number of white farmers killed. In July of 2012, Dr. Gregory Stanton who heads up the non-profit organization, Genocide Watch, carried out an investigative assignment in South Africa where he found that there is an organized campaign of genocide being conducted against white South African farmers.

'The farm murders, we have become convinced, are not accidental. It was very clear that the massacres were not common crimes, especially because of the absolute barbarity used against the victims. We don't know exactly who is planning them yet, but what we are calling for is an international investigation.' (47)

An investigation into South Africa, where we have the highest rape rate in the world. A country where public hate speech by black South Africans against white South Africans is increasing and is acceptable while much of it stems from powerful politicians.

Violence in South Africa is real. Racial tension is existent, and hatred towards white South Africans is genuine. Inequality and discrimination against white South Africans is real, and the failure to protect the minority is undisputed. Farm murders are occurring daily, along with increases in brutality and violence. The anti-white sentiment is authentic and brazen.

South African farmers are being stripped of the ability to provide for their families. We are being threatened with death should we not surrender our land, and a number of black South Africans have warned that they are coming for all that we own.

Waiting to be murdered in South Africa has become a new normal for my family and me. Waiting to be murdered in South Africa is a reality all our farmers live with as they await their turn.

We are asked why we don't simply pack up and leave South Africa? How do you ask a farmer to suppress his love for his land and reject his heritage? It is his birthright and was that of his parents before him. His passion for his farmlands was carried down by generations before him, and will seep over into his children who will, in turn, inherit his legacy.

Alice VL

But, what about the rest? What about my family or the families without the means to seek refuge somewhere else? What about the countries that don't want us, or are unwilling to acknowledge that the attacks on the South African minority exists?

We stay, and we prepare our children for what will inevitably come for us. We wait for our turn. We watch helplessly as the rise of political instability within South Africa translates to economic instability.

Where did that leave Zimbabwe when President Robert Mugabe's blatant hatred and racism towards white Zimbabwean farmers resulted in an annihilation of white people, and resulted in their subsequent fleeing from the country? It left them with hyper-inflation and massive starvation, which in the end, led to Mugabe pleading with the farmers he once expelled, to return just to feed the people of Zimbabwe.

My president refuses to recognize that the demographics and economic situation is almost identical. He won't hear or listen. He refuses to entertain the probabilities as the threat against farmers and white South Africans increase by the hour.

A selected few farmers who remain imperative to rebuilding the already-fragile economy in South Africa, consider

Alice VL

themselves defeated by the intended seizing of land, and are seeking lives and opportunities elsewhere. Those who *can*. Others are staying, preparing to fight for the land their fathers, and their fathers before them have farmed, nurtured, and loved.

But, the one common denominator between all white South Africans is the reality that we are not protected by our government. We are being brutally attacked and murdered on a daily basis.

Between 2010 and 2015, there were in excess of 2,500 violent attacks by black South Africans against white South Africans. The greater part of this number showed that they were tortured to death and suffered mental anguish by being forced to watch the gang-rape of their wives, daughters, and mothers. (48)

There is no official acknowledgment from my president that white farmers are more likely to be targeted for crimes, so the deaths of our farmers are being blatantly disregarded by the South African Police. The ANC government strongly denies that white South Africans are being intentionally pursued and persecuted and have stated that farm attacks and murders are merely a fraction of South Africa's wider violent crime problems.

Yet, we can't ignore the brutality of these attacks. We can't deny the growing rage of a community in South Africa that believes, without a doubt, we are being hunted, and then, terrorized. This forces us all to consider a new kind of normal for all white South Africans.

Our bedrooms are barricaded from the rest of our homes in desperate attempts to secure ourselves from attacks during the night. Steel gates are welded onto our bedroom doors, and then again, further down our passages to cordon off our vulnerability during the night.

Iron rods are used to cover up every single window, opening, and non-opening, in every single area of our homes. Our pets are brought in at night, and guard dogs patrol our grounds around our property. We can only hope and pray that they are not poisoned, stabbed, or shot during the night.

I know this isn't enough to protect my family. I know that our attackers can bypass any security measure I have in place, but perhaps, it allows me five minutes to respond.

I might have a moment where I don't wake up to six, or eight, or a dozen men standing around my bed as I stare down the barrel of a gun. What could I possibly do with those five minutes? I can't stop the attack. I can't defend myself, but, I can pray.

Alice VL

I know that when my turn comes, my beautiful, young, intelligent, respectful and Godly daughter will be the first to be tortured. The attackers will force her father to watch as they brutalize her. They will rape her, inflict pain on her, and quite possibly burn parts of her body before they murder a beautiful soul in cold blood.

They will come for me next. I pray they do. I could never get the images of what they will inevitably do to my daughter, from my mind. Death will be welcomed. Then, when I let out my dying breath, they will turn to my son, and terrorize and torture him for the next few hours. His father will continue to watch and die a thousand deaths while witnessing the brutality. It will crush him. It will slowly begin to kill him.

Once our attackers have snuffed out the lives of his family, they will finish him off. Perhaps, they will keep him alive to remind him of the attack for the rest of his life. But maybe, hopefully, they will murder him too.

Still, today, it wasn't my turn. It was someone else's. We remain anxious. Just a few days ago, a farmer received a tip-off of a planned attack on his farm. On the grounds of his lands, a crumpled drawing that resembled blueprints to his farmhouse was found. It clearly indicated the layout of his home. It itemized

Alice VL

that which was of value and more importantly, where their weapons could be located. The message on that 'blueprint' was clear, 'kill the Boer.'

He is edgy, disturbed, and apprehensive. Only the day before, a farmer a few miles down the road, was ambushed in his bed at 3am. But, before he was killed, as with hundreds of farmers before him, he was brutally tortured for hours.

He was burnt with a hot clothing iron, stabbed with a knife and cut with a blade. He was hit over the head with the arm of a pistol, over and over again. They stopped just moments away from him losing consciousness. The brutality of it all seems almost implausible.

Moments away from his own death, he watched helplessly as his son or daughter, wife or mother was beaten, raped and sodomised. There was nothing he could do to save his family. He was surprised by six barbaric intruders around his bed in the early hours of the morning. He had no chance, because, like the true cowards these attackers are, they came in numbers with stolen, automatic weapons.

It is not a fair fight for the farmer or his family. As he watched the lives slip away from every single one of his loved ones, he prayed for his own life to end soon.

Alice VL

What was rushing through his mind as he witnessed the rage, anger, and hatred reflect in the sadistic attack on his family?

Was the fight for land ever his fight to begin with? Was it fair to punish him for the so-called struggle that was never his struggle? Still, he was murdered simply because he was white, he was a farmer, and he owned farmlands.

In yet another farm attack in the community of a small, picturesque town in the eastern parts of South Africa, hundreds of locals had gathered together at the gate of Sue's Lynn's farm. Amongst them, was her husband, Robert Lynn. He stood up straight and held the hands of some in the emotional crowds around him. He was angry. His beloved wife, Sue Lynn, was brutally murdered, but he survived.

Armed attackers forced themselves into their home earlier in the year and began shooting at the sleeping couple through their bedroom window. Sue was hit and injured. After ransacking the house and torturing Robert by burning him with a blow torch, the couple were finally bundled into their own vehicle.

After driving almost 50 km's away from their home, they were dumped like trash at the side of the road. Robert was shot in the neck and survived, but he was unable to help his dying wife in the dark. With the bullet still lodged in his neck, his doctors know only one thing; he is lucky to be alive, and it's too dangerous to remove the lodged bullet.

Three men were arrested for the attack, but after the murder case-docket was destroyed in a supposed fire, the entire case has had to be recompiled. (49)

Then, there's the farmer in the Vaal area of South Africa. Three attackers broke into a 64-year-old woman's farmhouse and used an electric drill to sadistically torture her. When emergency rescue officials arrived on the scene, they discovered that all three her dogs had been shot and killed. The farmer was found lying in a pool of her own blood with serious head injuries, lacerations on her wrist, as well as numerous stab wounds to her feet. (50)

One case which really brought me to my knees was the gruesome murder of Deon Van Staden (51) and Babs Strecker (73) who were slaughtered in Bethanie, Northwest. Deon had multiple knife wounds and was bashed with a shovel at the back of his head. By the location of Babs' body, it was clear that she tried to escape to her bedroom and hide, but she couldn't make it out of her kitchen. She was stabbed and hit on her head with a shovel before their attackers fled in Deon's pickup with his 9mm pistol. (51)

Andre (Brood) van der Merwe (49) was shot four times on his farm by black attackers after he was tied up with barbed wire and dragged behind his bakkie, while still alive, for 1.5 km's. He eventually died from the injuries he sustained during the attack.

In 2015, the Swanepoel couple were tied to a single bed and tortured for hours. Their attackers took turns raping Rienie, while her husband was forced to watch the vicious assault. They then shot him in his leg when he began fighting back. A short while later, he was mercilessly shot and killed. Rienie was then forced to lie on her husband's body before she too, was killed. (52)

In 2010, the shocking Potgieter farm massacre horrified us all in South Africa. Attie Potgieter (40) was attacked by a gang of six black men when he arrived home. The attackers chopped the back of his head open with a machete and stabbed him over 150 times with a garden fork before he died from his injuries. In an execution-style murder, the attackers then shot his wife, Wilna (36), in the back of her head at close range. They then went on to shoot their three-year-old child, and before they left, they scribbled a message on the gate which read, 'We killed them, we are coming back.' (53)

Alice VL

What happened to the Fourie family in 2011 was inhumane and barbaric. John (77), and his wife Bina (76) died a horrendous death at the hands of four armed attackers. They were shot in their knees and tortured for hours before John was forced into the bathroom. The attackers shoved a showerhead down his throat before they poured boiling water down. At point blank range, they then shot him. His wife, Bina, was shot three times in her knees and in her back and left to die. (54)

In 2012, three attackers broke into a family home and gang-raped Geraldine (42), before they shot and killed her. They attacked her husband, Tony (53), with a golf club before shooting him in the head. Their son, 12-year-old Amano, was killed when the attackers tied his hands and feet, filled a bathtub with boiling water, and drowned him. The family dog's stomach was ripped open with a machete.

Five attackers carrying machetes, knives and a pickaxe brutally attacked another farmer and his family in 2014. The farmer was immobilized by being beaten, stabbed and skewered. Two of his attackers, who engaged in hysterical laughter, went on to urinate on him. He was then forced to witness the cruel gang rape and murder of both his eight-year-old daughter and his wife, before the men finally raped him. The attackers then cut his ligaments to prevent him from following them and left. (55)

Alice VL

Miss Lotter (57) was found with all her front teeth knocked out, and her entire body covered with bruises, chafing and stab wounds. She was sexually assaulted and mutilated with a broken beer bottle in her anus and vagina. She was so badly and barbarically assaulted, that parts of her uterus and cervix were missing, indicating that she was assaulted with a sharp object. Her injuries were so severe that the medical examiner was unable to tell if she had been raped by the two men, of which one of them was her gardener. Her mother Alice (76) had been stabbed in the neck and throat, and ultimately drowned in her own blood. The slogan 'Kill the Boer' was smeared in the women's' blood on the walls of their farmhouse. (56)

Dan Knight was violently killed in his Underberg home on the night before his 56th birthday. Beth Bucher was forced to watch as he, a lumber harvester, was bludgeoned to death by five attackers wielding hammers. With hammers and a monkey-wrench, he was beaten to a blood-splattered pulp. (57)

In another horrifying farm attack in Lichtenburg, 73-year-old Elizabeth Kotze was stabbed to death with a knife, before her body was mutilated. She was gored several times as the attackers disfigured her face when they cut out a large cross. (58)

Johan Strydom (40) was attacked on his farm by three

attackers who shackled him to his pickup and hauled him behind it. During the court hearing, it emerged that he was quite possibly alive before being dragged behind the pickup, and subsequently died of a burst liver, and cracked skull. A journalist had quoted one of the attackers as saying he was 'proud of what he had done.' The same attacker was arrested and released a month earlier for attempting to kill another farmer. (59)

Heila Killian (63), was killed when five masked attackers shot her at a braai (barbeque) on a friend's farm. They then made off with two rifles, one shotgun, and a handgun, as well as a white Toyota Hilux pick-up. (60)

A brutal farm attack took place on a farm in Kuilfontein, Groot Marico near Zeerust, in the North West province. Hans van Loggerenberg (72) and his wife were attacked during broad daylight on a Monday morning in July 2018. Hans had his skull broken after it was hacked open from repeatedly being hit over the head. His severely traumatized wife locked herself in the bathroom and sought help by means of an emergency radio. (61)

An elderly white couple, both in their 70's, were attacked and tortured on a smallholding just outside of Krugersdorp on the West Rand. An unknown number of attackers entered their home, and brutally assaulted them. The elderly man, who is bedridden, couldn't get out of his bed during the attack. They tortured him by pouring boiling water over him, while intending to burn the elderly woman with a hot iron but fled after taking a firearm and money. (62)

Around 11pm on a Saturday evening, the emergency network of the Drakenstein Farm watch received a call from a farmer's wife, frantically informing them that a farm attack was in progress. The farmer, a friend, their wives, and children were enjoying an evening braai on their porch.

The farmer, an active member of the Drakenstein Farm-watch, and active in firefighting, medical care, and armed response. He was painfully aware of the dangers of living on a farm and was as prepared as he possibly could be. When two attackers were spotted behind a wall, he ordered his family and guests inside their house to secure the doors, and to lock down the premises. His wife immediately used their emergency communication which is recorded at the Farm-watch control-room. At that stage, the situation was unknown, and the number of attackers was not clear. When the two men, the farmer, and his friend, went to investigate, they were immediately confronted by two attackers pointing firearms at them. One of the attackers tried to fire off a shot, but inexplicably, it did not go off. Fearing for their lives, the farmer returned fire before the attackers ran off to the adjoining buildings. (63)

A farmer (87), his wife (84) and their twenty-year-old grandson were attacked in their home when attackers gained entry through the back door of their home. The attackers forced their victims to the floor and battered their grandson. Weapons and jewelry were taken during the attack. (64)

Stefne Evans (60), was struck over her head with a brick during a home invasion in Bathurst and died at the scene. Her partner was injured during the attack. (65)

Boet Smal (70), was stabbed in his head and chest, and died in his house on a smallholding in Heidelberg. His wife Esther (60) was stabbed in her back. (66)

Marie Venter (74) was murdered in her home in Reitz. Her bloodied body was found by her children the following morning. (67)

Sonja Joubert, a friend of Jasper von Kleist (61), who was shot and killed during a farm attack in March 2018, showed the Freedom Front Plus (FF+) around the bloody scene where the attack took place, and said that it hardly seemed as though their attackers intended on stealing anything. Jasper Von Kleist, the manager of the farm Dale in the Tom Burke region, died of gunshot wounds to his upper body while Sonja was shot twice; once in her arm and another in her shoulder. She had little doubt that their only intention was to shoot and kill the white residents on the farm. (68)(69)

Hester Hooper (58) was severely attacked, assaulted, and raped by an attacker in her home on a smallholding in Deneysville at approximately 10pm. She was at home alone when she was alerted to an unfamiliar noise outside her home. When she switched on the outdoor light, she detected a possible intruder near her home. She tried to contact the police but dialed the wrong number since the known emergency number had recently changed. The attacker flung a brick through a window of her home, climbed in, and attacked her before he raped her. (70)

In March 2018, Dirk Steenkamp (71), a large cattle farmer from Vredefort, Free State, was shot dead outside his house before his attackers fled without taking anything. Dirk was armed when he left his house early the morning to investigate a faulty water pump. This was, however, the sixth attack on his life. (71)

In Alexandria, Eastern Cape, Near Grahamstown, farmer Riaan Scheepers was left seriously injured after being beaten when two of his trucks were stolen. Riaan, (62) a cattle farmer of 27 years, died in the hospital after the attack. (72)

Alice VL

Loutjie Erasmus was shot dead execution-style shortly after midnight on July 2018 on his friend's small farm, Rooigrond in Lichtenburg. It was later found that robbery was not the motive for the attack; his vehicle was still running when his body was discovered. (73)

Gert (78) and Pauline Smuts (71), their son Louis (47) and wife Belinda (42) were all murdered when their attacker locked Belinda up, went over to Paulina and Gert's house, and shot Paulina in her face. He pulled out her nails, raped her, and then shot her in the head. He then waited for the men to return before shooting them both in the head. He then returned to Belinda demanding her bank card and PIN number before shooting her in her head. (74)

During the early hours of a Sunday morning in July 2018, a farm manager was found lying on his bedroom floor, bleeding profusely from a wound to his head. According to his wife, they were asleep in their bedroom when attackers broke a window, and demanded they open the door. When her husband climbed out of bed, shots were fired which struck him in the head. The bullet went through his skull and has resulted in the permanent loss of his eyesight. (75)

A farm attack took place in July 2018 in De Wagensdrift,

Cullinan, Gauteng. A 19-year-old man was shot in his chest by an unknown number of attackers when he went out to feed animals on their smallholding. (76)

Another farm attack took place in July 2018, in Boshoek in Limpopo at approximately 2am. Four attackers armed with pistols, tied up a man and a woman, before assaulting them. (77)

In June 2018, a farm attack took place at Mooiplaats, east of Pretoria in the Gauteng Province. A woman was attacked by one male attacker after which her handbag and purse were stolen. During the assault on the woman, she was stabbed in her hand with a screwdriver. (78)

Another farm attack took place in June 2018 on a smallholding in Bokfontein in the North West. A man and woman were attacked after three attackers gained entry to their home through a back door. The couple were forced into their bedroom and tied up. They were both attacked by a panga. He sustained injuries to his head, and her to her hands. (79)

Choppie Bruwer (78) and his wife Marian (68) were shot in the head execution-style while tied to chairs in their house on their farm in Van Stadensrus in the Free State in June 2018. (80)

A sadistic farm attack took place on a farm in Van

Stadensrus, Free State when a couple was murdered in the early hours of the morning. They were aged 68 and 78 years old and were both AfriForum members. Their safe was found open, and their vehicle was missing. Their domestic worker later found their bodies. (81)

A man was killed after being stabbed in a robbery on a farm on the corner of Annandale Road in Stellenbosch in June 2018. When paramedics arrived at the scene shortly after 4:30 pm, they found a member of a security company performing CPR on him. He was stabbed with an unknown object in his chest, and after continuous resuscitating efforts on him, he eventually died of his injuries. (82)

Another violent farm attack took place in Rustenburg, North West province, in June 2018. A farmer, his wife, and children were attacked by five armed attackers. During the attack, the farmer was shot and killed before they fled the scene in the family's white Toyota Fortuner.

During another violent farm attack, a prominent strawberry farmer from 'Mooiberge Strawberry Farm,' Jeffrey Zetler (62), who supplied both Woolworths and Pick n Pay, was stabbed to death. (83) The attack took place in the offices of his farm in Stellenbosch, Western Cape in June 2018. By then, Zetler had survived four prior attacks.

In the early hours of a morning in June 2018, a family was attacked in Leeuwfontein, Roodeplaat, Gauteng. Jonty Jacobs (28) heard attackers trying to break in, and force entry through a window. When he shouted out to them, he was shot twice through the window. His 6-year-old daughter and his fiancé witnessed the shooting.

Just after midnight, a couple living on the farm Blombos were awoken by a loud bang. They then discovered that their bedroom window had two bullet holes, and upon further investigation, found a small projectile on their bed, possibly that of a .22 rifle. (84)

An 85-year-old woman was attacked in her home in June 2018 at approximately 9am. The farm attack took place at Duiwelskloof, Modjadjiskloof, Limpopo. She was overpowered and assaulted by her attacker before he fled with a chainsaw. (85)

In another incident, a group of three men wearing balaclavas gained entry to a farm when they attacked and restrained a security guard by tying his hands and feet, before they made their way to the farmhouse. They ordered a man who was outside, inside the house where they tied his hands and feet. When they found a woman in the house, they tied her up next to him. They then fired off shots, hitting their male victim once, and the woman several times. The man was later certified dead at the scene by paramedics. (86)

A manhunt was launched by the police in Modimolle after a farm attack in June 2018, at around 8am. The couple in their 70's was sitting inside their car when four armed attackers emerged from the bushes and confronted them. They demanded money and, in the process, the woman, Lesley van Niekerk, was shot while still sitting in the pick-up. The attackers then fired shots at her husband who was not struck. (87)

In one incident, Marie Venter (74) was cruelly assaulted, raped and murdered on a Friday night in June 2018 in her home in the Reitz area. (88)

Kobus and Marlise van Niekerk were attacked at their farm in the Reitz district at 4am one Sunday morning. Marlise was hit with an unknown object and forced to open the safe in their house. (89)

In June 2018, a 70-year-old farmer was attacked by four armed attackers. They forced him into his home, and robbed him of jewelry, four firearms, a Ford Ranger pick-up and an undisclosed amount of cash before they fled the scene. (90)

Another victim was shot dead on a smallholding in Hillside near Randfontein on the West Rand in May 2018. Two men were asleep at home when one was woken up by a strange noise. He immediately awoke the second man and found attackers fleeing their home. The first man then gave chase after the intruders but was later found with a gunshot wound to the head. The 23-year-old victim was rushed to the hospital but died before he could be airlifted to another hospital, leaving the second man severely traumatized by the incident. (91)

A couple was attacked on their smallholding in the Colleen Glen area outside Port Elizabeth in May 2018 at approximate 7 pm. Their dog was restlessly sniffing at the door and disconcerted by something when the 79-year-old went to investigate. When he opened the door, he was overpowered, and forced back into his home. His wife (74) tried to activate the panic alarm but was overpowered by the attackers before she could. They were then tied up and restrained before the attackers plundered their home, and gained access to the safe, stealing two firearms, jewelry and cash before fleeing the scene. (92)

A gruesome farm attack and murder on the farm Welgevonden near Poortjie on the West Rand took place where Fanie (78) and Colleen (74) Engelbrecht were brutally murdered on Mother's Day in 2018. Fanie's throat was slit, and Colleen was mercilessly strangled with an iron cord. (93)

In May 2018 at approximately 4am, a farm attack took place at Marula Oase, Bela Bela in Limpopo. Christo Janse van Vuuren and his wife were attacked by four attackers when Christo opened the door to check on a noise he had heard. He sustained a serious knife wound; the attackers fled without taking anything. (94)

In May 2018 at 7:30 pm, a farm attack took place on a farm in the Donkerhoek area in Rustenburg in the North West. Andrè Pretorius was overpowered by three armed attackers at the gate outside his home. They forced him back into his home where two more attackers were waiting. They severely assaulted him, and tried to restrain him but failed, and fled the scene with his firearm and cell phone. (95)

Dries Schoeman (70) and his wife Mariaan (68) were attacked with an angle iron on their farm Skoongezicht outside Machadodorp, Mpumalanga. Dries was brutally murdered while Mariaan survived, even though she was viciously attacked and suffered serious injuries. Mariaan arrived home at 4pm when she was attacked by four attackers. She was beaten with a sharp object and tied up with wire. When Dries arrived home approximately an hour later, he found his wife covered in blood.

While untying her, he too, was attacked from behind. Dries was inhumanely beaten with an angle iron, and suffered severe head wounds. After he had been tied up, the couple were dragged into the bushes, and left for dead. Mariaan managed to free herself the following morning, and summoned help. Dries died two weeks later in hospital from the monstrous assault. (96)

An elderly farmer and his wife were attacked on their farm in Bela Bela, Limpopo in 2018, at about 1 am. Their attackers gained entry to their home by breaking down a security gate and a door with a crowbar. The couple who are in their seventies were assaulted in their bedroom and tied up with pantyhose. Their son arrived to help after the man was able to summon help by freeing himself at around 3 am. (97)

A farm attack took place at 7 pm in May 2018, in Elandslaagte in KZN near Ladysmith. The farmer, Charles Carbutt, was away visiting his daughter at the time that his workers were attacked, restrained, and a number of firearms stolen. The farm workers, a husband, and wife, heard dogs barking at around 7 pm, and upon investigation, found five attackers who, after tying them up, robbed them of cash and cell phones. One attacker stood guard while the others ransacked the farmhouse. An angle grinder was used to free the safe from the prefabricated wall, and then used to slice open the back of the safe. (98)

In May 2018 at 4 pm, a cattle guard was severely injured when he was attacked with a panga in Ogies, Mpumalanga. The farm worker was attacked next to the cattle kraal, where his home is, and where the attackers were attempting to steal the cattle. After calling for support from fellow workers, the attackers fled leaving the victim with serious panga wounds. (99)

A group of four attackers attacked the farm Heuningspruit near Kroonstad in May 2018, at 11 am. The farmer's wife, Hantie Lotter, and farm workers were assaulted and tied up. Tewis Lotter, the farmer, was not home at the time of the attack. One of the workers who resisted the attackers was severely assaulted. Following the assault, Hantie opened the safe and firearms where the attackers took all the cash. (100)

In a farm attack in the Rankins Pass area in Limpopo in May 2018, at approximately midnight, two farm workers were tied up, before shots were fired at a whiskey farm manager. He was assaulted and attacked with a panga and sustained wounds to his leg. (101)

An elderly Free State couple were violently attacked by six attackers on their Langeveld farm in the Hertzogville area in April 2018 at 7 am. Japie van den Berg (75) and his wife Emma (75) were confronted outside their farmhouse by six attackers and forced back into their home where they were robbed of two firearms. (102)

Dudley Foster, who was admitted to the Intensive Care Unit in April 2018 after a brutal farm attack, remained in a critical condition after he was viciously and repeatedly stabbed. His partner Annie said that it was 'touch and go' for a while, but that he was eventually stabilized, and survived the attack. He sustained seven stab wounds and was struck over his head by a bar stool. The three attackers wore balaclavas; one was armed with a knife, and the other two armed with handguns. (103)

In April 2018, an elderly woman (60) was attacked on a smallholding outside Vryburg in the North West. Four attackers gained access to her home before strangling and threatening to stab her with a screwdriver. She was immensely traumatized after enduring the violent attack. (104)

A family has been dreadfully traumatized after a violent farm attack on a farm in Boshoek outside Rustenburg in the North West at 3 am in April 2018. Three armed attackers surprised a 26-year-old man while he was asleep in bed. His pregnant wife, their 1-year-old child, and 11-year-old child were tied up and restrained with wire. The attackers were armed with a shotgun and a pistol. Mrs. Motha, his mother, was shot in the head during the attack. (105)

Another brutal farm murder occurred in April 2018 on Spioenkop farm, Umhlali, KZN. Mr. Govender (77) and his 70-year-old wife were attacked at their home at Spioenkop farm when three attackers gained entry to their house. They had dug in under the electric fence to gain access to the property and were armed with knives. Mr. Govender arrived home at about 9 pm and was confronted by the attackers when he opened the door to his home. His and his wife's hands were tied behind their back while Mr. Govender's legs were tied together, they were forced to endure a violent assault. His wife died in the attack. (106)

In April 2018, between midnight and 2 am, seven attackers armed with knives overpowered Christo and Lizel Bosman on their farm. The farm is situated between Kuruman and Hartswater in the Northern Cape. Christo was stabbed and admitted to a hospital in Kimberley. (107)

The body of an Eastern Cape farmer (62) was found near his farm next to the roadside outside King Williams Town. A friend of the murdered farmer who had monitored his vehicle noticed that his vehicle was stationary outside his farm. It was only after he went to investigate that he found his body. (108)

In April 2018, at approximately 1 am, seven attackers

attacked a farm in Bokfontein in the North West. Two of the attackers gained access to the house by opening a sliding door and removing the bolts that locked the gate from the inside. They then opened the doors inside the house by removing the hinge pins. They were armed with tonfas (police-style batons) and a sjambok. They brutally attacked a woman and her 9-year-old and 13-year-old daughters by repeatedly hitting them over their heads and their bodies. (109)

In a farm attack in Mamogaleskraal near Brits in the Northwest in April 2018 at approximately 10 pm, four men aged between 25 and 55 were attacked and tied up by six attackers, two of which were armed with firearms. One of the men was stabbed in the leg with a knife, and another was stabbed in his back and chest. (110)

In Joubertina, Eastern Cape, an elderly farmer (74) was severely assaulted with a snooker cue in March 2018 at 7 am. Two attackers gained entry to the farmhouse through a window, severely assaulted the elderly farmer, and fled the scene with nothing more than a handbag. (111)

Chris du Plooy (80), a farmer from Paul Roux in the Free State, was brutally attacked on his farm Rexford in April 2018 at 4 am. 'The man was attacked and overpowered whilst he was asleep, he was stabbed, assaulted and interrogated by two suspects. The attackers dragged him from room to room in search of money and firearms whilst they ransacked the house. A shotgun, revolver and a cell phone were taken. The suspects then tied him to the bed and fled the scene,' Police Spokesperson WO Lorraine Earl said. (112)

Phillip Long and his stepson, Timothy, were attacked on his farm in March 2018, in Franklin, Kwazulu Natal. When Phillip arrived home after 10pm that evening, three attackers were waiting outside for him. They beat him up and gained entry to his home, where they frantically began searching for money. Timothy, who had been asleep, was also assaulted after being tied up. (113)

During an attack at Heuningkloof farm in Hackney in the Eastern Cape in March 2018, a woman (44) was shot in her lower back and raped in front of her young children. The children were tied up with wire before an attacker raped their mother. The attacker screamed out in anger that he intended to slaughter the entire family after being fired by her husband. (114)

Three masked attackers smashed their way into a home on a smallholding in Bushy Park, near the Lavender Barn in Port Elizabeth. The men armed with a crowbar, a firearm, and a knife attacked the elderly residents, a couple aged 78 and 79 years old, along with the woman's sister of 85. The crowbar was used to beat the man over the head, crushing his skull. The woman and her sister were severely traumatized and locked in the bathroom. (115)

In another incident, a farm manager (40) had his hands behind his back with wire before being repeatedly stabbed and hacked by attackers. His wife was raped by the attackers. He was then dragged 100m from where they were initially attacked and hung by a wire by his feet after which he was stabbed until he died. (116)

Martin Louw (59), a well-known farmer in the area of Tulbagh, was stabbed to death in his farmhouse in March 2018. (117)

On the same day, a woman (62) was attacked on her farm in the Moorreesburg area. (118)

In the early hours of the 14 March 2018, a family of six were attacked and robbed at their smallholding outside Centurion, an area where there is constant and heightened tension with regard to illegal land invasions. The attack happened at about 1am in the Knoppieslaagte area between Olievenhoutbosch and Erasmia. Ian Cameron of the lobby group

Afriforum said, 'Five armed men gained entry to the house via a glass sliding door that they broke open. A man and a woman in their sixties, along with their two children in their twenties and two primary school children, a boy and girl, live in the house on the smallholding.' The attackers overpowered the family in separate rooms and tied them up before they spent over an hour rummaging through the house. The young woman was sexually assaulted in front of her 5-year-old son during the attack, and only managed to free herself at about 2am to call for assistance from the Afriforum neighborhood watch. This was the second attack on them in seven months. (119)

The Groblershoop police in the Northern Cape are investigating a case of murder after the body of a woman (65) was found in February 2018. 'The woman was home alone, and it is speculated that she had been assaulted and strangled.' Captain Jaques September said. The victim's bank cards, and cell phone were stolen during the attack. (120)

The body of a woman (72) was found murdered in her home on a farm near Chrissiesmeer, Mpumalanga in February 2018. She was found in the bathroom where she had been tied up. (121)

A farmer from Lichtenburg in the North West was

attacked and robbed on a Sunday in February 2018. Dirk (69) and his wife Lettie Pretorius (56) had just returned from church at noon when they were attacked by three attackers. 'The three suspects gained entry to the house where they severely assaulted Dirk with a stick and their fists. They beat his entire body but mainly his head.' said Lt. Col Amanda Funani. (122)

A 73-year-old man and his family were watching television on a farm in Charl Cilliers near Secunda in February at approximately 10:30 pm, when three attackers carrying firearms stormed in. They demanded their safe keys and forced the man into his bedroom. After he handed them the safe keys, they shot and killed him. Before they fled, they shot and killed his two dogs who were in the house. (123)

An 82-year-old farmer and his wife from a farm near Windsorton were asleep in February 2018 when attackers entered their home, assaulted them, and tied them up. (124)

An elderly couple were attacked in their home on a farm in the Reitz area in the Free State in February 2018. The 76-year-old man was dragged to a bathroom during the attack and assaulted with knobkieries. He subsequently suffered severe head injuries. (A knobkierie, also spelled knobkerrie, knopkierie (Afrikaans) or knobkerrie is a form of club used mainly in

Southern and Eastern Africa. Typically, they have a large knob at one end and can be used for throwing at animals in hunting or for clubbing an enemy's head. The knobkierie is carved from a branch thick enough for the knob, with the rest being whittle down to create the shaft.) (125) His wife was detained in another room where she was able to call for help at around 6:30 am when the attackers finally fled. (126)

Berdus Henrico (39) was shot during a farm attack in Limpopo in February 2018. The bullet barely missed his aorta when it found its way through his jaw and exited out the back of his neck. Berdus and his fiancé were attacked by three armed attackers on a farm outside Vaalwater at about 9 pm. They were alone in the house on a farm in the Melkrivier area where Berdus manages the farm. Berdus and his fiancé fought back, and were subsequently assaulted and shot three times. (127)

Shortly after 12 am on the morning of 9th February 2018, Netcare 911 responded to reports of a home invasion on a farm in Hekpoort, Gauteng. When emergency services arrived at the scene, they found a 21-year-old man who had sustained serious injuries to his face, as well as a stab wound to his back, and a woman who had been assaulted. Three armed attackers entered their home and attacked the young couple. (128)

A 64-year-old woman, Wilma Liebenberg was attacked on a farm in Kalkfontein in Groblersdal in February 2018. It later came to light that the attackers received information about the farm from attackers who struck the same farm in 2012. Kobus Liebenberg, Wilma's husband, said that his wife was alone in the farmhouse at the time of the attack since he worked in town during the week. According to him, she went to bed at approximately 11:30 and was asleep when their dogs, who were sleeping with her in her bedroom, began to bark agitatedly. She got out of bed and noticed that the passage light on the top floor was on. She took her revolver and fired two shots through her bedroom window. She then noticed the light go off and heard someone walking down the stairs. When they banged on her bedroom door, she fired shots through the door. The attackers dragged their injured accomplice out of the house and helped him over the three-meter-high wall where they dragged him for about 15 meters, before simply leaving him. (129)

Kotjie Conradie (83), and his wife, Tienie (79), were attacked by four armed attackers in February 2018, at around 3 pm when they arrived at their farm Uitijk which is situated between Aliwal North and Burgersdorp. The couple had dropped off their farm workers in Aliwal North before they returned home. They were assaulted and forced to open their home and their safe. The attackers fled in their Hilux pick-up with an unknown amount of cash, firearms, and a cell phone. (130)

Just after 2 am in January 2018, an armed robbery took place at a farm on Driefontein road, Muldersdrift in one of the cottages where three attackers held up a man and his wife. The man was shot in the upper part of his arm, while the woman shot in her stomach. (131)

A farmer in Broederstroom, Willem Joubert (37) went to check on a beam activation when five attackers assaulted him. He was then shot in his upper body. They tried to drag him up the stairs into his home, but in the end, left him next to his swimming pool. His sister (40) locked herself in the house and activated their panic alarm. She escaped through the back door and ran to the staff for assistance who escorted her into a field where she hid away. (132)

In February 2018, a farmer and his wife were attacked on their farm in Vryburg by two attackers armed with knives. Horrifically, the farmer's fingertips were bitten off in the attack. (133)

A family from Kriel in Mpumalanga lost their home and possessions after their house was set on fire shortly after a robbery one Monday night. Larry Cronje, a wheat and cattle farmer, said that he and his wife Jana, and their four young children were away on holiday near Pongola in Kwazulu-Natal when they received a call alerting them to the fire at their home. Larry said that an unknown number of attackers, who according to the police were searching for money, had forcefully entered their house. He said the police suspected that the attackers set the house on fire since they could not access the CCTV footage and were in all probability afraid of being identified at a later stage. After the attack, the Cronje couple and their four children plan to emigrate to Canada. (134)

Police were called to a smallholding in Grahamstown during the afternoon of 3 January 2018, where two attackers were arrested. Shortly after 5 pm, local security officers responded to a panic alarm, and called the South African Police Service for backup. On entering the house, they found two attackers between the ages of 18 and 26 inside, while two people aged 70 and 75 were found severely beaten on their smallholding. (135)

Jacques Bouwer (42) and his son Jan (17) were attacked and stabbed by three attackers on the farm Maraisdal, near Caledon. The attackers gained entry to their home and stabbed Jan in the back while Jacques was stabbed in his hand. (136)

Alice VL

Another male victim was shot and killed while responding to a neighbor's call for help with a robbery in progress on a smallholding situated in the Doornradies area, Tshwane. The attackers held the family hostage in their home while they ransacked their property for valuables. When the neighbor approached them armed with a shotgun, the attackers shot and killed him. (137)

Despite more than 346 farm attacks so far for 2018, Bheki Cele, our Minister of Police, still refuses to declare farm murders priority crimes. This does nothing more than leave South African farmers to accept the reality that our president is deprioritizing farm attacks and farm murders. (138)

As we try and come to terms with all these attacks and murders infiltrating our homes and our lives, we are faced with the fact that our Land Affairs Minister Maite Nkoana-Mashabane was quoted as saying, 'white people should also stop taking up land that belongs to Africans at the cemeteries. They should go bury their loved ones overseas where they came from.' (139) (140) Where do I come from? Where do my children come from? Where do the Boers come from? South Africa is where we come from. This is where generations before us are buried.

The number of farm attacks, home invasions, hijackings,

and murders, are exorbitantly high in South Africa, despite the fact that our government claims it is at an all-time low. Despite the blatant way in which my president announces to the world that there are no farm attacks. Not surprising, since most attacks aren't reported, and those that are, are summarily re-routed and re-classified as normal crimes. My government is telling the world that farm attacks are purely crimes of opportunity due to the remoteness of farmers. They say that attackers specifically target farmers because of 'chance.' They say that these attackers are able to apply brutal torture tactics to farmers and their families since they are so remote, and without security companies and neighbors to provide quick response and assistance.

But that is not true. The truth is that farmers are being tormented and murdered at an alarming rate in an effort to 'reclaim' land that was supposedly once stolen from black South Africans hundreds of years ago.

We are hated. Despised. Loathed. We are branded as substandard citizens who will soon be left homeless. In the words of black South Africans, the idea is to cleanse the country of all white citizens and reclaim land that was stolen from black South Africans.

Alice VL

Black First Land First (BFLF) leader Andile Mngxitmana, announced after a meeting that land, on which whites have built homes, is stolen land, and that white South Africans must pay reparation fees. 'We want them [whites] to pay a reparation fee for using our land. So, in other words, if you are a white person and you have a house, fine, no problem—but you must pay the rent to the rightful owners of the land.' (141) He went on to say that all land in South Africa is stolen, and that it must be returned to black South Africans.

The truth is, the South African farming community has suffered attacks for many years. The majority of the attackers have been young black men, and the majority of the victims have been Afrikaner farmers. While the government describes the attacks as nothing more than part of the 'bigger picture of crime' in South Africa, we point to brutal attacks and incidents involving self-declared anti-white motivations as evidence campaigns to drive us from our land.

For decades, South Africa was the focus of an international rallying call against the inequalities of apartheid. In 1994, Nelson Mandela and the African National Congress (ANC) assumed the reins of power in South Africa. The international community looked the other way. They were satisfied and happy that justice had finally triumphed.

Alice VL

Today, they continue to look away, even as South Africa disintegrates into a brand-new racist pit where Afrikaner farmers have accepted the fact that is politically correct to murder white South Africans.

For a while, the ANC banned crime statistics from being compiled, let alone published. They claimed that they would scare off foreign investors, and boycott investments. (142) But, the world knows very little of the savagery and brutality that accompany these killings. Many of these victims, including women, children, and infants, are raped and tortured before they are murdered.

From boiling water being poured down their throats, to being burnt, hacked to death with machetes, or disemboweled, we can't deny the absolute savagery and barbaric ways in which these crimes are committed.

But, is the Government truly complicit in these murders? What other conclusion can we make when we are faced with our then-president Jacob Zuma who led and sang the song, 'Dubula iBhunu' during the celebrations which took place when the ANC celebrated their 100th year anniversary. 'Shoot The Boer' forms part of the lyrics of an apartheid-era and struggle song called 'Ayesaba Amagwala' which translates to 'The Cowards Are

Scared.' This is unmistakably in violation of the South African Constitution that prohibits the advocacy of hatred based on race and constitutes incitement to cause harm. Yet, these songs are provocatively sung almost daily. These chantings are shown to create a hype, and illicit a brand-new wave of attacks and killings. These songs are the messages these attackers are waiting for; it is *okay* to murder. It is seen as permission to go forth, kill the Boer, and make it someone else's turn.

In January 2012, then-president Jacob Zuma was on record as publicly singing, 'We are going to shoot them with the machine gun. They are going to run. You are a Boer. We are going to hit them, and you are going to run. Shoot the Boer.' (143)

Again, is the government complicit in these murders?

When white South African protestors calmly and peacefully urged the South African Minister of Police, Nathi Mthethwa, to allow the murders of farmers the same level of urgency as is given to rhinoceros poachers and copper cable thieves, Zweli Mnisi, Police Spokesperson spoke in absence, and accused the protesters of 'grandstanding.' 'They are only representing people based on their color. For us, racializing crime is problematic. You can't have a separate category that says, farmers are the special golden boys and girls. You end up saying the life of a white person is more important. You cannot do this.' (144)

Yet, according to Johan Burger, a Senior Researcher with the Pretoria-based Institute for Security Studies' Crime and Justice Program, white farmers' concerns are legitimately distinct. He said that it is currently twice as hazardous and treacherous to be a farmer in South Africa, than it is to be a police officer in this country. He found that the global murder rate in the country is 31 per 100,000 people, and yet my government assures the world that our murder rate is at an all-time low.

The murder rate for police officers is 51 out of 100,000, but for farmers, who are overwhelmingly white, the rate climbs to 99 out 100,000. (145)(146)

At a conference in 2011, Julius Malema, Leader of the Economic Freedom Fighters, was once again in full swing with his proposed plans. He complained that South Africa's 'willing-buyer, willing-seller' program wasn't working. The program which is aimed at redistributing a third of white-owned land to black South Africans was a failure. 'You can never be diplomatic about willing-buyer, willing-seller. It has failed. You have not come up with an alternative. We are giving you an alternative; we must take the land without payment.' (147)

Alice VL

Carte Blanche, South Africa's Investigative Journalism Program, has since directly linked Julius Malema to white farm murders in South Africa when the program hosted a Sunday-night special dealing with farm invasions and land expropriation issues in South Africa. (148) This included a leaked audio tape from an interview with a gang member recruited by the EFF to attack farms and farmers.

In a presentation on the gruesomeness of attacks on white farmers, a man can clearly be heard speaking in Afrikaans where he confirms that Julius Malema was committed to helping him continue cold-bloodedly murdering farmers as soon as he is released from prison.

How can it be that Julius Malema along with his racist outbursts and threats, not only against white South Africans, but world leaders; his contempt for the law, firing off an AK47 in public and his public hate-speech, does not even raise an eyebrow?

How do we even begin to carve out a future while all this is thrown at us, from every single direction?

Alice VL

WE WILL NEVER BE READY FOR THIS

"Oh no … we were not ready for this!"

My greatest frustration lately is the words, "Oh no … we were not ready for this!" When asked where I come from, the response is almost always the same, "Wow! Lucky you! What a beautiful country! What lovely people!" or "Oh, that's where Nelson Mandela won his struggle for freedom." *But*, the response I get all the time is, "What a pleasure to meet someone from a country that has overcome apartheid."

I am always stunned by the reality that nobody really knows much about South Africa. Actually, I am flabbergasted and slightly disgusted. I so desperately want to blurt out that we have *yet* to overcome apartheid – we *haven't*, but for the players that have changed.

And then it happens; I want the world to know. I want this sweet grandpa standing in front of me to know. I want the lady who has just asked me to sign a book, to know all about the barbaric and sadistic killings of the minority in South Africa.

Alice VL

Quite often, I am nudged and signalled to pick my words carefully, and not say too much. It's upsetting, they say. People can't digest such cruelty, they say. People just aren't ready, they say.

But, I can't keep quiet, and once they've formed a picture of the heartless and evil killings of white South Africans, they stare at me in disbelief, and shockingly utter the words, "Oh no, we were not ready for this," before they hastily excuse themselves, and head out in the opposite direction, afraid that they might 'catch the killings' – as though it is contagious. As though it will now invade their lives.

"Wait. What? *You* were not ready for this?"

How do I tell them that *we* weren't ready for this either? How do I explain that those tortured and murdered weren't ready for their worst, but living nightmares? The father whose eyelids were removed, forcing him to watch his wife and daughter raped, wasn't ready for this *either*. The mother, who listened to the screams of her daughter being brutally gang-raped, and the choking sounds a little boy made while boiling water was poured down his throat, wasn't ready for any of this.

How do I tell them that nobody is ever ready for any of this, yet, *we* are forced to live this? How do I get them to understand that when four or eight attackers burst through the windows and doors of a home, there is no negotiating? There is no postponing or re-scheduling an attack on them. There is no option to walk away. There is never an opportunity to inform their attackers that they 'are just not ready for this.'

How do I tell them that the scenes they play out in their minds can barely compare to the reality these families were forced to endure, before they ultimately die at the hands of evil? How can they understand that not *one* name on those crosses in a field in South Africa, was *ever* ready to come face to face with the devil?

That little boy drowning in boiling water wasn't ready for this. The mother of a 9-year-old princess wasn't ready to hear her daughter's screams while being chased and hunted through the corridors of her own home by her very own bogeymen. When a 2-year-old little girl is picked up by her blood-soaked feet after witnessing the brutal slayings of her parents; when she is held up by her beautiful red locks, shot through her head, and tossed into a box, she wasn't ready for this either. When a young lady in the prime of her life pulls off to the side of the road on a busy highway to change a flat tyre, she certainly wasn't ready for her attackers that came out of nowhere and snubbed out her life.

Alice VL

So, while the world sleeps without having to check their doors and windows over and over again each night; while the rest of the world tosses and turns about their plans for the next day, perhaps looking forward to a planned holiday, or reminding themselves to schedule a meeting later in the week, maybe quickly working on a budget for a new car while choosing a school for their youngest or considering a college for their eldest, someone in South Africa is facing their greatest fear, and they are *not ready* for the evil the darkness brings into their home.

Somewhere in the darkest of the night, a little boy is listening to his mother begging for the lives of her children. A little girl is desperate for her daddy to save them. A mother is trying to put on a brave face while she knows she is moments away from taking her last breath. A father, desperate to fight off their attackers and save his family, is confronted with a dark, demoralizing reality; he is *failing* his family. It isn't a fair fight. It isn't his fault. It will never be his fault but still, they weren't ready for this. Nobody will ever be ready for this. So, instead of walking away from the stories you aren't ready to hear, consider those that weren't ready to live it.

Alice VL

HOME INVASIONS

'A blueprint to a home invasion.'

When hand-scribbled notes were found on a man shortly after his arrest, residents in Chatsworth were horrified by the revelation that they were being 'watched.'

Moorland Place near Demoroza School Unit 9

No alarm

No security

Retired man with his wife. Got lots of money saved in his house.

He sells gold chain, ring, lamp – tops

Go very slowly.

Threw cilling (ceiling)

Some gold kept in the outbuildings

Go threw cilling (ceiling)

Alice VL

Come 2 morning

No alarm

No security

Hit wife

She give you everything

Take his cars

Every Wed wife go 10 clock

Come back 1 clock

Break kitchen door in the side (149)

While our farmers anxiously await their turn in farm attacks and murders, the remainder of the minority in South Africa wait for our turn to come in equally brutal home invasions.

In Statistics, South Africa's recently published annual victims of crime survey (VOCS), just over 128,000 households experienced home invasions where attackers made physical contact with residents during the period of April 2016 to March 2017. (150)

Markings to houses for intended invasions is not

confirmed, but neither denied. The South African Police Service cannot confirm or deny the use of house markers to point out houses that are being targeted for home invasions. (151)

However, South African Police Captain Dingaan Motsamai gave a presentation and explained how a 'Z' painted on a stop sign, piles of stones, and strategically placed crisp packets outside gates were signs left by criminals watching a house ahead of an attack and home invasion. The secret code of attackers who target suburban homes has since been translated by police and shared with the public to help prevent attacks before they happen. (152)

Despite our efforts to keep our heads down and prevent these attacks, we are still limited in defending ourselves when it comes to firearm control. Obtaining a firearm license is intricate. While it is a right to own a firearm in most countries, it is by no means at all, a given right in South Africa. Our legislation is aimed at limiting handgun ownership by implementing licenses and regular renewals. (153)

As many as 400,000 firearm owners who failed to renew their firearm licenses in time, were forced to hand their firearms over to the South African Police as they are now deemed to be in illegal possession of weapons. In June 2018, The Constitutional

Court upheld an appeal by the Minister of Safety and Security, dismissing a high court order which had declared that two sections of the Firearms Control Act of 2000 were constitutionally invalid. The sections concerned were the expiration and renewal of firearm licenses. Under the previous Act, a license to possess a firearm was indefinite. The Act of 2000 changed this. Under the new administration, each person who intends to own or possess a firearm must first produce a competency certificate which expires after periods of two, five or ten years, depending on the nature of the firearm license. (154)

Our president and our ministers are safely protected and guarded in their homes while millions of South Africans live in fear of being targeted and murdered in what is supposed to be the safety of their homes.

An annual report released by the South African Police Service concluded that there is only one police officer for every 369 South Africans which suggests that our police force is critically understaffed. (155)

Armed home invasions are barbaric and sadistic, resulting in traumatic experiences that occur with consistency in South Africa. These are often violent and occur at any time of the day. In many cases, attackers infiltrated the homes of their intended victims when they are home simply so that valuables and weapons can be located with ease. But, we know that, as in the cases of farm attacks and murders, these attacks are racially motivated, especially when the cruelty and gruesomeness of these assaults are later brought to light.

Even more chilling is the fact that the laws in South Africa make it almost impossible for residents to protect themselves during an attack. Being confronted by an attacker does not give any South African the right to defend ourselves by any means necessary. The law is clear, we cannot shoot an intruder or would-be attacker just for trespassing or gaining entry to our homes. If an intruder is unarmed, we, the residents, would then be in serious trouble should we inflict harm on a would-be attacker.

In fact, we are only permitted to defend ourselves if the attacker(s) are armed and are threatening to kill or seriously harm us. In other words, we may defend ourselves when it is almost too late. 'Self-defense action must be relative to the circumstances of the attack' according to the Constitutional Court. If an attacker or intruder is armed with a knife, and we are convinced that they will use it as a weapon to inflict harm, we must use appropriate force, appropriate force and not excessive force. (156)

Alice VL

Home invaders shot and killed a 64-year-old father in the Hartbeesportdam area one Saturday afternoon, as he desperately tried to his daughter from harm. He was frantic to negotiate with the three attackers to let his daughter go when they shot him in the chest. He died at the scene, but his daughter managed to escape and seek help. (157)

Residents at the Margate Retirement Village were left reeling in shock after a 76-year-old resident was taken to the hospital after being attacked and robbed at the retirement home. She said that the attackers tied her up and demanded money from her. While tied up, they assaulted her, resulting in severe injuries to her face. (158)

Three men forced their way into a home in Jeffreys Bay and assaulted a woman one Saturday morning. They hit her over her head with an unknown object before taking an undisclosed amount of cash, jewelry, and clothing before fleeing her home. (159)

Rosalie Bloch, 84 and Aubrey Jackson, 94, were found tied up and murdered in their Victorian double-story home in a quiet suburb of Rosebank, Cape Town. Their bodies were discovered at about 9 am by a relative who was due to pick them up. (160)

A businesswoman was shot and raped at her home outside Hankey in the Eastern Cape. The 44-year-old woman was shot and wounded when an attacker fired several shots through a glass door to gain entry just before midnight. She was then forced to drive to an ATM in town to withdraw money. While the attacker was withdrawing cash, she managed to get back into her vehicle and drive to a nearby farm in the area before alerting the police. According to AfriForum's Head of Community Safety, Ian Cameron, the woman was raped during the attack, which he said was carried out by more than one attacker. 'Her children were tied up, and the attackers also threatened to hurt her daughter. She talked the attackers out of hurting the children, after which they hurt her.' (161)

A prominent Durban businessman who was shot and wounded during a robbery at his Westville home was admitted to hospital in a stable condition in the Intensive Care Unit. Imraan Randeree, of Randeree Jewellers, survived the shooting, but his mother-in-law, Rookaya Dhooma, died at the scene after two attackers shot them during a robbery at about 9:30 pm. (162)

Deon van Wyk, a volunteer with the Kruin Community Voluntary Association, said that Andrew du Plooy had opened the back door of his home to let his dog out when he realized there were strangers on his property. He tried to get back into the house, but a shot was discharged, and it struck him in the upper stomach. His wife managed to secure herself and their children in a bedroom before the attackers tried to get to them. They subsequently fled with a television, a laptop, a handbag, and other household items. (163)

A man, aged 28, two teenagers and two children were sitting in a vehicle in Brown's Farm when three armed attackers fired at them before fleeing the scene. The man, the teenagers, and a 12-year-old child died at the scene, while the second child was injured and rushed to the hospital. (164)

16-year-old Franziska Blochliger was raped, robbed and murdered in Tokai, Cape Town, in what was deemed as a vicious, callous and cruel attack. (165)

Student Hannah Cornelius and her friend, Cheslin Marsh were accosted and kidnapped by a gang of men while they sat in her car in Stellenbosch. Cheslin was stoned, stabbed, and left for dead. The attackers drove Hannah to a paintball range, where they raped and killed her. (166)

A member of the Vryheid community policing forum says the attack on Bokkie Potgieter, aged 73, who died after being repeatedly hit with a panga, was so brutal that his face was left unrecognizable. His father said that after the attack, the attacker dragged the dying elderly man by his feet and shoved his body head first into his own pickup before he drove off with one of Bokkie's feet dangling from the window. (167)

Nico Rautenbach was brutally assaulted during a house robbery in Garsfontein while preparing for a church service. The Afrikaanse Protestantse Kerk reverend got up early to prepare a sermon, as he normally does. He was savagely beaten when attackers hit him with torches over his head, punched him to the ground, and kicked him. When his wife went downstairs to intervene, she was met with a gun that was pointed at her head. They then assaulted Elsie, and forcefully removed her wedding ring from her finger. The attackers then ransacked the house, took a television and a laptop while Nico was still being assaulted outside. (168)

Amanda Groenewald, aged 59, woke up around 1:30 am in her home in Wilgehof, Bloemfontein, to two attackers standing next to her bed. She spotted the cable ties they were carrying that were already looped and knew at once that the attackers knew exactly what they were going to do. They pushed her around and began strangling her. She says she realized that she should not fight back and pretended to be unconscious. The attackers then ransacked her home and made off with cash, a ring, and a cellphone. (169)

Alice VL

Ronald Moreland, aged 46, was murdered in a security-gated complex in Olympus, Pretoria. He was alone and worked from home. His wife Lize found his severely beaten body on the lawn when she came home from work that evening. Although he was covered in blood, nothing was missing from their home. (170)

Two attackers marched into the bedroom of Dillon Barnard (21), who was sleeping with his four-month-old baby and shot him a number of times. He died at the scene; the baby was only grazed. (171)

Hetta Potgieter (84) was found dead in her frail care apartment in Nelspruit. Her hands were tied behind her, she was raped and strangled. (172)

Ann Smit (86) was found lying in a pool of blood in her home after a violent attack. She died in Greenacres Hospital from head injuries sustained in the assault. (173)

Frik Botha (82) was murdered in his home in Garsfontein, Pretoria. He was beaten to death with a metal pipe. (174)

Rev. Braam van Wyk (80) was kicked in his face, and his hands were tied behind his back. His good friend, retired Professor Kobus Naude, was murdered by their attackers who stabbed him with a knife through his heart. They fled with Rev.

Van Wyk's white Mercedes Benz. (175)

Jan Lombaard (50) was shot and killed by a group of five attackers in his home in Leeudoringstad in North West. His father, Henk, was viciously assaulted by the attackers. (176)

Crystal Dawson (28) ran through bushes and an electric fence to flag down motorists after her father, Peter Dawson, was shot and killed by three armed attackers in their house in Broederstroom. (177)

The end goal for each South African is to survive a home invasion without spending the rest of our lives in prison for defending ourselves, our families, or our property. We can't simply react out of fear. The legal system is adamant that we calculate the risk of harm by evaluating an intruder's actions as opposed to the consequence of our defensive actions. Then, we need to establish the likelihood that an attacker will, in fact, cause harm to our families. Only once these points have been checked off, will our defensive actions be considered as reasonable force.

It really doesn't matter where in South Africa you live; home invasions happen so often that it barely even reaches news outlets anymore. We might get a glimpse of invasions when there are multiple murders, or a level of brutality and gruesomeness involved.

A home invasion is one of the most frightening and dangerous crimes to live through, especially when they come in at night, and show up in numbers. The horrifying reality is that it violates our safe place, the one place we think of as our sanctuary.

But, what leaves us entirely defeated is the fact that an arrest is made in only one out of every five reported cases of home invasions. And after that, only one in five people subsequently arrested for a home invasion, is convicted.

We keep vigil and listen for unfamiliar sounds. We keep a lookout on the streets in front of our homes, and we cut away plants, trees or bushes that might allow an attacker to hide and wait. And tonight, when the sun sets, my fear will once again overwhelm me. Just as every night before this one, I will hand my daughter a doorstopper fitted with an alarm. Once her bedroom door is securely locked, I will slip one in under all out-going doors and finally, lock myself in my own bedroom and wedge in my own doorstopper. I am constantly aware of the fact that as I lay asleep and as my daughter sleeps, we are vulnerable in our beds. Our safety measures are not enough. They never will be.

The attackers have no fear of being caught or of being

Alice VL

stopped. They will not be stopped. They will not be thwarted. Tonight, in the darkest hours of the night, I will lay awake and pray that it is not my turn, and that it's not my child's turn.

And, when tomorrow comes, I will berate myself because, while my turn didn't come, someone else's did.

Alice VL

Alice VL

THE HAUNTING OF SOUTH AFRICA

Tears Of an Expat

We dream of taking just one more walk through our lands, cross over our deserts, and stroll carelessly along our shorelines. We hunger to climb our hills, saunter below our mountains and barefoot, we are desperate to feel the beaches underneath our feet. We want to rush in underneath a waterfall, paddle through a river, and wade our toes in our oceans. We long to watch the sun set and the sun rise again over our valleys and seas, and step in under the rain that comes crashing enthusiastically down from our South African skies.

Instead, we emerge from our nights of hiding, reminded that we have reached just one more day to fight, and one more night to survive. Our respite is short-lived when we hear of another farmer dead, another mother lost, another child fighting for his life and another home destroyed. Another family wrecked. Another heart lost. Another soul broken. We are faced with homes in ruins, some riddled with bullet holes, each telling a

Alice VL

story of fear, brutality, anguish, and death. History that has been preserved in buildings for centuries are burnt to the ground, expunging a little more of our heritage and our past. What has stood agelessly now lies ruined at our feet. Our hearts try to bravely recover by telling our minds that it was only a building and that no matter how hard they tried, they could never erase our history from our hearts or from our minds.

Sometimes, we are numb, we don't cry. Sometimes, we see and we hear, but still, we don't cry. We simply bend our knees, lower our heads, and thank God that our family was sheltered and are safe, *for now*. We breathe a little easier and when we hear that another home was brutally invaded, we hold each other a little tighter. We are beleaguered by guilt because it was someone else, and not us. We hate ourselves for the temporary relief of surviving another night, when someone else didn't. We hate that in the darkness, the ghastliest of nights for someone else, their terrified voices echoed out into the distance, praying and begging their attackers for mercy. In silence, we live their last night. We don't say it, but we live their anguish, and we feel their suffering. We step carefully into their lives as details of their cruelest night reaches us. We know one thing; we are not as brave as they were. Another family wrecked. Another heart lost. Another soul broken. Death reaches us all, but how we are reaching our end is grueling. How we end up praying for death to show up, is excruciating. How the pain, torture and barbarism inflicted upon us, is dispiriting, leaving us with no other option or wish other than to invite the mercy of death into our homes. In that moment of torment and despair, we are no longer attached to our lives, our homes, our possessions, our friends, our sanity, our heritage, our culture, our family, or the lands in which we have invested our hearts in a country our souls used to dwell in. A thousand different ways before that night, we have tried to count the ways in which we have remained devoted to our country, yet, the magnitude of our adoration for our homelands will never matter again. For those who have stood at and walked through death's door; for those hiding in the night, South Africa will always be our greatest love story, our greatest sadness, and our greatest consecration. Our commitment to our God is that which built a bridge between our souls and our country, one that will always be home to us, to our hearts, and to what is the very core of us.

We sit and think. Sometimes, too much. Sometimes, too wildly. Sometimes, too overwhelmingly. Sometimes, we are crushed. Sometimes, we want to hurt back. We want to punish those who don't walk like we do, who don't believe as we do, who don't feel as we do, and who would never pray as we do.

Alice VL

Sometimes, we just sit and think, and sometimes, we just cry. Sometimes, we are enraged, and we want to discard the banner used to conceal the hurt and harm they have caused us and our tribe. We want to fly high our flag again; a cloak once worn by South Africa to remind us of who we are, and how God called upon us to be courageous and to love all. One where we could stand stripped and naked under our stormy skies, and still be covered and clothed by our flag. And, as it flutters in the wind, we come alive again. As we stand fascinated by the vision before us, we once again see the symbol of our country's love and devotion to us. One, where our nightmares are over, and where our dreams can breathe again. A place where we are asked only to worship our God before our nation, and then, to stand together under our homeland's cape as it nudges us towards its promises and allows us to take another walk through our lands, across our deserts and along our shorelines.

We don't know how to ask for help anymore, or where to turn to any longer. Nobody wants to know. Nobody wants to hear. Nobody wants to see. But us. *Nobody wants to.* We can't stand to watch the pain and destruction around us, so, like the strangers we have become, we leave. We walk slowly beneath unfamiliar skies and down city streets that we know; carry no evidence of the lives we had once lived. As deep into the soils as we could dig, the grounds in a strange land would never find the preservation of our footprints we left behind in the soils when we were only children. It would never know *of* us, even if after a while, it gets to know us. We could never love with our soul, for the pieces we have left are barely enough to allow us to breath the air of a country that didn't raise us.

We hear the way others speak around us, and it leaves us feeling conquered. We listen for the language of our kind, but no matter how desperate we are to hear sounds like ours in a crowd, it remains silent. We search the masses for the faces we love, and the souls that we have left behind. Sometimes, when we find ourselves wandering around aimlessly, we are so sure we hear a voice that we once knew, only to discover that it was no-one at all. It was nothing more than a hankering, a whisper from the soul.

We once used to lay awake at night, waiting for the voices and the shadows of the night to come for us, now we lay awake, haunted by the mutters of our oceans, rains and winds back home. Nothing is the same anymore. The sounds of the rain crashing down on our streets, sidewalks and lands has a rhythm and a song of its own, and the way our skies darkens during our thunderstorms is something we have not yet seen since. Our backdrops, our mountains, our hilltops, our bush, our forests, our thunder and lightning, our sunsets and our sunrises, will always be like nothing we have ever seen, or will again.

These are all the pieces of us left behind in a country we never wanted to leave. The power and beauty, the glory that rests on the strength of our flag and our heritage is not ready to welcome us home yet, back to our homelands. We pray each night that our beloved South Africa keeps our hearts intact, until we can come home again.

Alice VL

HOME & LAND GRABS

At the ANC's 54th annual conference, South Africa's majority ruling party made a decision to formally adopt a policy that would allow for the expropriation of land from white landowners without compensation. During President Cyril Ramaphosa's February 16th State of the Union address, he said that the ANC government was committed to accelerating the land distribution program in order to right the wrongs of the past. (178)

South African lawmakers voted 241-83 on a motion that would begin the process of a constitutional amendment that would make it possible to confiscate land from white owners and transfer it to black South Africans without any financial compensation whatsoever.

In August 2018, City Press reported that the ANC had identified 139 farms for expropriation without compensation, and that the National Executive Committee had resolved to amend the constitution to expropriate land without compensation.

Alice VL

'We must ensure that we restore the dignity of our people without compensating the criminals who stole our land,' South Africa's President Cyril Ramaphosa said. (179)

Bluntly stated, he claimed that farmers are criminals who stole land, and that it is imperative to resolve racial inequalities in land ownership. Yet, throughout the world, there is not much sympathy for South African farmers. 'There is a severe ethnic hatred seeping through observations in The Star, controlled by Zuma minion Iqbal Survè,' – Veteran Journalist Ed Herbst. (180)

The land expropriation policy of South Africa's ruling party, the ANC, will explicitly target white South Africans according to Zweli Mkhize, the Minister of Cooperative Governance and Traditional Affairs. 'Not the property of black South Africans, nor land controlled by traditional leaders would be targeted.' (181) (182)(183)

The ANC government, one who has a long-standing and intimate relationship to the South African Communist Party, is an Afro-Marxist party that has threatened to nationalize all farmlands in South Africa for years. The government has subsequently met with councils of the National House of Traditional Leaders over their apprehension about the intended redistribution process, Zweli Mkhize said in an emailed statement. 'A wrong impression has been created that the discussion on land expropriation includes land in the hands of traditional leaders.' The Zulu king Goodwill Zwelithini has threatened to secede if land given to his tribe by the country's previous white government were to be expropriated.

In 1994, shortly before the ANC's occupation and rule of the country, the Zulu land was placed in the Ingonyama Trust, presided over by the king. President Cyril Ramaphosa stated that such land under the trust 'would remain untouched.' 'We have no intention whatsoever to even touch the land engaphansi kweNgonyama under the Ingonyama Trust,' President Ramaphosa said. (184) 'There will be no smash and grab.' (185)

Home and land invasions have become predominantly more newsworthy in light of political events in South Africa, but in all reality, it has been going on in South Africa for years. Long before parliament's recent vote in favor of the expropriation of land without compensation, land-grabbers have been clashing with the government for access to land even though they have been fairly consistent in dismissing these actions as nothing more than prosecutable criminal acts.

Yet, black South Africans are of the opinion that the ANC has given the go-ahead for land expropriation without compensation, thus ensuring land-grabbing has more or less been given another green light.

My president is currently engaging in a fierce publicity campaign where he paints pictures of unity and fair land issues, while doing so behind the masses of the 'previously oppressed,' and therefore, placing more and more South Africans at risk. (186) He has explicitly guaranteed that the expropriation of land without compensation program will not harm the economy or the agricultural sector at all, as it did in Zimbabwe. Yet, Zimbabwe presently relies on international aid to feed growing numbers of its population, according to the World Food Program. (187)

Bluntly speaking, land grabs without compensation, and transferring white-owned land to black South Africans to enable them to become property owners is nothing more than state-sanctioned theft and all this while we, the white South Africans are expected to continue to pay our mortgages even after the land is taken from us. (188)

When a Malawian foreigner defied protestors in the recent Hermanus land-grabs, her house in Zwelihle Township was burnt down, and she lost everything. 'There were stones on the road, and people were protesting. I woke up on Saturday and things were worse. We were told we could not go to work, but I had to go.' (189)

In July 2018, in an up-and-coming mobile residential compound on Gauteng's East Rand, suburban bliss had turned to a living hell when what was referred to as 'building hijackers' had methodically begun to take over one unit after another while openly refusing to pay rent, levies, and municipal services. (190)

A British farmer residing in Muldersdrift, was arrested on charges of attempted murder when he fired off shots with a paintball gun into the ground to warn a trespasser (or what some speculate to be a would-be-land-grabber) to leave his land. He asked the trespasser to leave his property, and warned him that he was trespassing, but the intruder refused. 'Politely, I asked him again to leave my property, or I would call the police and have him arrested for trespassing.' The man replied, 'The police would never arrest me. I'm going to take your farm.' He then slowly made his way towards the property owner who then took out his paintball gun and pointed it to the ground. Later, the owner was informed at the Muldersdrift Police Station that the man he accused of trespassing had opened a case of attempted murder against him, and that he would be arrested. Police then placed the owner under arrest where he was held behind bars for the night. (191)

Alice VL

In Haniville, Pietermaritzburg, a vacant field was littered with glass bottles, trash, and paint where land-grabbers were marking out spaces to build their homes on. Hundreds of people from Haniville, Copesville, and Sobantu areas occupied the vacant land which is owned by the local municipality. Many of them expressed their frustration and have become impatient with the government's failure to provide housing.

Siyabonga Nkosi, one of the illegal occupiers, said, 'I've been renting in a shack for years. When I came back from work on Saturday, people were already cutting the land. I saw people choosing spaces, and I joined them. I now have my site for my home. We need land, and we are taking it.' (192)

Carrie Esterhuizen and her two children aged four and eleven months, were in a hostel at the Cremona Cheese Factory in Tshepisong, Johannesburg, when angry land-grabbers set the building alight on a Friday afternoon in May 2018. She said she could smell the petrol bomb as she called her husband for help. 'I tried not to think about the petrol bomb and focused on getting my kids out of the house.' (193)

Corby Hill Estate and Donalds Saints Farm in Eshowe were under attack in KwaZulu Natal, South Africa when a mob carrying pangas and machetes burnt down farmhouses, workshops, farming equipment, and torched thousands of hectares of sugar cane crops. One farm was completely burnt down, and the other was still burning when residents were continuously battling to get emergency services to respond.

Scores of land-grabbers participated in what was deemed to be the largest land invasion Buffalo City Metro, East London had ever seen. They illegally earmarked government and private plots along the Buffalo Pass route and the R72, just outside Cove Rock near East London. To mark off their territories, they used tree stumps and red tape. The land grabbing began with several local people leading the pack. Others came from nearby communities. Many also came from afar to identify and claim their portion of the property. (194)

Despite the illegal land-grabbing taking place throughout South Africa, my president is pushing ahead with plans to amend the constitution to allow for the expropriation of land without compensation. While addressing the nation, President Cyril Ramaphosa said the ruling ANC government will finalize a proposed amendment while will allow the transformation which he says is of 'critical importance' to the economy and will 'boost food security and tackle inequality.' Without formally amending the constitution, the farmer of the first South African farm prepared himself as best as he could to have his land seized without payment or compensation. He was quoted as saying, 'Whichever way they dress it up, it is theft.'

Johan Steenkamp, who co-owns a R19 million hunting farm in the Limpopo province, was ordered to hand over his land, following a ten-year battle to stop the government from purchasing it for a measly tenth of its value. He was quick to accuse President Ramaphosa of the fact that redistributing his land is nothing more than a façade to cover up the fact that valuable coal deposits can be found under his farmlands. (195) Given President Ramaphosa's previous directorship at Lonmin Mine, it is not impossible to consider that there may be darker financial motives to 'expropriating' the first farm. (196)

In 2014, after Cyril Ramaphosa became South Africa's Deputy President, the Register of Members' interests, tabled at parliament, revealed that his wealth was believed to be $550M (R6.4 billion). In addition, he owns thirty properties in Johannesburg and two apartments in Cape Town. As of August 2017, he owned approximately a hundred Ankole breeding cows at his Ntaba Nyoni farm in Mpumalanga. (197)

SUBTLE INTIMIDATION

A Thorn in The ANC's Side

Steve Hofmeyr is one of South Africa's best-known singers and songwriters and is also known for his acting career, writing, and poetry. He completed two years of compulsory military service before joining the Pretoria Technikon drama school.

He starred in the 1990 Franz Marx film 'Agter Elke Man' (Behind Every Man) and in 1992, joined the cast of M-Net's flagship soap opera 'Egoli: Place of Gold.' He is also known for his role in 'Treurgrond' (2015) which depicts a typical farm murder in South Africa, and 'A Case of Murder' (2004).

In 1997, his music career took off when he recorded a duet for his album 'True To You' with Belgian superstar Dana Winner, called 'You Don't Bring Me Flowers.' Steve won SAMA (South African Music Awards) for Best Selling South African Artist in 2003 and 2004.

Alice VL

In 2006, he hosted his own show on Afrikaans channel kykNET, called 'Dis Hoe Dit Is Met Steve' (That's How It Is With Steve).

But first and foremost, Steve Hofmeyr is an activist for white South African farmers, and has openly voiced his concerns and displeasure at the government's inability to protect its farmers, and subsequently, protect the white citizens of South Africa against genocide. (198) (199)

He has made numerous claims relating to the murders of minority South Africans. He has openly claimed that white South Africans, and in particular, Afrikaners, are being 'killed like flies,' and has regularly posted on social media that 'my tribe is dying.' (200) He posted a picture to social media of a World Cup soccer stadium, which he claimed could be filled by the number of white South Africans murdered by black South Africans. (201)

But, his attempts at creating awareness for a vulnerable community has come at a steep price for him personally. He was branded as a racist when in October 2014, Steve Hofmeyr wrote and published a tweet stating that he believed that black South Africans were the 'architects of apartheid.' This prompted a significant public backlash. One of Hofmeyr's critics was puppeteer Conrad Koch, and through his puppet Chester Missing, he launched a campaign calling on companies to boycott their sponsoring of Steve Hofmeyr. (202)

Steve Hofmeyr has *accurately* given statements indicative of apartheid denialism, leading various journalists and political analysts to label him a 'disgrace to South Africa.' He was quoted as saying that he could trace his African roots further back than Economic Freedom Fighter leader, Julius Malema could. This led to several festivals and events boycotting the star. (203)

Steve Hofmeyr has been branded a racist simply because he is unapologetic when it comes to defending the Afrikaner South African, and campaigning for the rights of white South Africans. He is branded a racist for publicly and *accurately* pointing out that white farmers are murdered by black South Africans.

He is branded a racist for his role in exposing genocide in South Africa and speaking up on behalf of minority South Africans. He has admitted to getting up to seven death threats an hour. Steve Hofmeyr has shaped a level of anger amongst black South Africans with his penetratingly angry outburst over Willemientjie Potgieter's execution, and the murders of her parents. (204)

A chilling message was written in Sotho on cardboard at

the Potgieter home, 'We have killed them. We are coming back.' This message was found on the gate of the farm where three people were brutally killed in 2010. The victims of the murders were Attie Potgieter, 40, his wife Wilna, 36, and their 3-year-old daughter Willemien. It was surmised at the time that little Willemien was shot so that she wasn't able to identify her parents' killers. Three farm workers were arrested and later, in townships in the area, three more suspects were arrested for the murders, one which was only 17 years old. The Potgieter family were murdered in their home on their 11th wedding anniversary. Arno Potgieter from the neighboring farm, Van Tondersrust, spoke about the murders of his brother, sister-in-law, and Willemien, 'It is still half unreal. It was a terrible, terribly big shock.' After her mother was killed, 3-year-old Willemien was presumably taken to an outside room and shot in the back of the head.

The body of Willemientjie as she was fondly known, was then carried to her mother's body in the main bedroom where her mother had been shot in the back of the head. Willemien's body was found with a pink ribbon still tied to her hair. In the house, a plate of food was in the microwave. Attie's body was found outside his home, next to a fence at the back door. He was presumably surprised and hit on the back of the head with a sharp object, possibly a panga, and in addition, he was stabbed with a garden fork.

When reporters arrived at the scene, his body was covered by a pink blanket, where he died. Giving testimony, pathologist Dr. Robert G Book said that Attie had 151 stab and laceration wounds. Wilna's injuries revealed several deep lacerations to her head and a gunshot wound to her neck. 'Indications were that the woman and child were shot at close range,' he said.

When asked by state prosecutor Jannie Botha on his first impressions of Attie's body, he said that the deceased 'had been tortured to death.' He said the injuries could have been caused by tools such as a garden fork, panga, spade or sharp knife; other injuries could have been caused by a brick or stones. The State alleges that the six attackers assaulted Attie outside his house with knives, a garden fork, and a panga, killing him. They then attacked Wilma and Willemientjie inside the house before shooting them. (205) (206)

Steve Hofmeyr directly blamed the 'propaganda of entitlement' amongst black people for the brutal massacre. He was quoted as saying, 'I don't know how the world thinks we (the Afrikaners) can transform, integrate and let go of our prejudices and stay nice, tolerant Christians when blacks can shoot a 3-year-old child in the head.'

Threats against Steve Hofmeyr became public after voicing his disapproval of the brutality of the Potgieter murders. One threat against Steve Hofmeyr was from Noxolo Nox Sebe, 'I'll be very happy if someone kills Steve Hofmeyr. His racist anti-black attitude and behavior are irritating. Now he is accusing us (blacks) of being killers of white farmers. Fuck him, because white people were the ones who stole our land and wealth and murdered millions of our people in the name of civilization ...'

Zama Kwela wrote, 'I agree that white swine must be killed!' (207)

Lola Bam wrote, 'Steve Hofmeyr has declared war against us. I agree with Skhura; either he goes to Australia, or he perishes!' (208)

When asked by Yolisa Mkele if he was a racist, Steve responded with, 'I'm being called a racist every time I distinguish between races, but I see it as being racial. We made it taboo to even distinguish between white and black.' (209)

In 2017, a concert in New Zealand that would feature Steve Hofmeyr as one of its headline acts, was canceled following pressure from South African expats angered at his inclusion. (210) Johan De Villiers, who is based in Amsterdam, said that 'on receipt of the information detailing Hofmeyr's controversial comments and positions on various issues, there was a cancellation.'

Earlier in 2017, a concert by Steve Hofmeyr which was initially scheduled for February 11th at the Nederburg Wine Estate was canceled after an appeal to the estate by Johan De Villiers to 'scrap the event.' (211) It was later revealed that these cancellations and subsequent boycotts were due to nothing more than the fact that Stever Hofmeyr continued to sing 'Die Stem' (South African National Anthem prior to 1994) which was supposedly 'insulting to black South Africans.' (212)

One of the largest South African Festivals Steve Hofmeyr has been banned from is Afrikaans Is Groot. This occurred when Pick 'n Pay, and Jaguar Land Rover South Africa decided not to renew their sponsorship of the Afrikaans Is Groot concerts. (213)

Klein Karoo and Innibos Arts Festivals have said that Steve Hofmeyr abused their platforms for his own opportunistic political propaganda, and that they don't want him back. (214)(215)

This was all for the singing of Die Stem. 'Die Stem van Suid Afrika' is a poem which was written in 1918 by CJ

Langenhoven, a great Afrikaans writer, and cultural leader. Music was later added to the poem that speaks of the beauty of South Africa and the devotion to making South Africa a better country. Die Stem became the national anthem of the Union of South Africa in 1957. The song is included in the FAK songbook and is seen as a cultural treasure of the Afrikaans language. (216)

This all for campaigning and advocating against the ANC government regarding the murder of white farmers. This all due to his fervent attempts at creating awareness of white genocide in South Africa. By holding onto and fighting for the survival of his and the Afrikaner heritage, Steve Hofmeyr has been accused of 'taking various steps to spread racial hatred and commit defamation against black South Africans.'

In 2016, Café Dudok, a restaurant in the Netherlands, refused Steve Hofmeyr, though he had been scheduled to give a talk about the 'future of Afrikaners.' Cafe Dudok barred him from the premises after being made aware of Hofmeyr's so-called 'white supremacist views.' (217)

In 2016, The Cape Town Press Club invited Steve Hofmeyr to deliver a speech, but due to threats by leftist' groups, his invitation was retracted.

Below is an extract of his speech which points to South

African genocide.

10. I believe we are trying to bury the dangers of black violence by saying things like 'Black Lives Matter,' 'Blacks Can't Be Racist' and then failing to publish crimes along racial lines as they do worldwide. The countries of our (white) European descent sport a 2/100,000 murder rate. South Africa, besides being the rape capital of the world, also sports a 33/100,000 murder rate; so don't mind me if I tend toward paranoia when farm murders occur at 5 times the national average (more than 150/100,000) which is already 5 times the world average and 15 times the European average. You can make me go away if you prove these trends wrong or present me with the fact that whites are responsible for these statistics and that therefore black appeasement and white punishment is generally justified.

11. I am not sorry at all if I believe that these staggering rates are genocidal. I am not sorry at all that I said that my people simply are not used to these levels of rape, by others, on us. Everybody is free to determine their own tolerance and threshold to these brutalities. The common answer I get is that whites are murdered less than others (as if that satisfies our new threshold) or that we are all victims. Yes, this we know, but are we all perpetrators? We will never know. The point here is, if I'm wrong, and we overreact, we will solve it, and if you as a liberal

Alice VL

are right and we under-react, you will get the statistic you deserve. Which is the hardly-bearable status quo.' (218) (219)

Given Steve Hofmeyr's active campaigning against what the government calls 'Alleged Boer Genocide,' he has been labeled a racist and accused of creating panic amongst white South Africans and subsequently, barred from various national and international events.

Steve Hofmeyr says, 'In 2014, I was banned from singing a song that is not banned. After banning me from singing Die Stem, appearances and festivals in association with the ANC and DA (not all) excluded and banned me. So have radio stations owned by the ANC. Speedily, this resulted in me losing thousands in income. It was Nelson Mandela himself that decided not to ban Die Stem. He would probably have known how childish it would be. Of course, songs can and should be banned. Songs such as Kill The Boer that entice citizens to murder the opposition. Who doesn't understand what? Die Stem is a song that asks for peace within a nation and homeland. It asks for prayer in thanks.' (220)

Not so Subtle Intimidation Anymore

Until recently, silencing Steve Hofmeyr has been relatively subtle; tactful, delicate, diplomatic, discreet, cautious and understated.

Until recently.

2019 has seen an overwhelming attack on his freedom of speech, his music, his right to stand up against corruption, his livelihood, and has resulted in a series of injunctions, snubs and sanctions against him as a singer, entertainer and activist for the Afrikaner tribe.

Companies such as AIG (Afrikaans Is Groot), MTN, Toyota, Media 24, DSTV, only to name but a few, have withdrawn their 'association' from him resulting in a nomination for a Ghoema award being summarily withdrawn. The songin question is Die Land, performed with four other singers. This supposedly as a result of a statement he made in 2014; (Excerpt) He was branded as a racist when in October 2014, Steve Hofmeyr wrote and published a tweet stating that he believed that black South Africans were the 'architects of apartheid.'

Yet, here we are, exposed to hate speech, threats and promises to cease our lands by the South African government including Cyril Ramaphosa, Julius Malema, and the cronies of BFLF. Cases of hate speech, incitement to kill, violation of human rights etc. are all disregarded by the South African or rather, the ANC law because it is acceptable behavior.

Alice VL

It is honored by our law that the minority South Africans, yes, the white South Africans are guilty of being white and that we, the Afrikaner tribe have no rights. Struggle songs calling for the slaughter of our tribe is up to the standard of the ANC government, Toyota, DSTV, MTN, AIG, Media 24 and so on, because we are white, we are hated, and we do not matter. It has once again become clear that there is a direct attack on the Afrikaner nation, our music, our right to function, and our right to life.

Alice VL

VIOLENT PROTESTS & VANDALISM

South Africa is known as 'the protest capital of the world' with one of the highest rates of public protests. As of July 2018, South Africa has experienced 144 protests since January 2018, the latest data released by the Municipal IQ showed.

The worst affected province was the Eastern Cape, followed by Gauteng. There was a slight increase in protests in the Western Cape and Free State. 'The footprint of protest activity is increasingly evident across a diverse range of communities - from cities to rural areas, with the range of issues including growing demands for housing and job opportunities in urban areas to basic services and better governance in smaller municipalities,' Karen Heese, an economist at Municipal IQ, said in a statement. (221)

A library worth close to R2m was torched and burnt down during protests in Ixopo, the KwaZulu-Natal Department of Arts and Culture has confirmed. The modular library in KwaNokweja, was apparently close to completion when it was burnt down. The government had spent R1.9m on the building which was fitted with a study area and provided free internet. It would subsequently have accommodated up to a hundred students at a time. It would have had the capacity to house three thousand library books and materials. (222)

Residents in Hermanus were imploring the South African Army to assist the South African Police in dealing with the violent protests, but their requests were denied. Forty-two protesters were arrested during violent clashes with police officers after hundreds of protesters from Zwelihle torched the Hermanus swimming pool facility.

Hermanus, in the Western Cape, still resembled a scene from a horror movie days later due to ongoing violence, intimidation, and political upheaval, damages were estimated at around the R50 million mark. When speaking to residents, it was clear that there was much more to the actions than what the media had reported. Over and above the violence and destruction, there was an undeniable level of intimidation.

Businesses could not function since staff and employees were not permitted to leave the township. School-going children were compelled to pay to be allowed to attend school but had to report back to the leaders of the uprising before 2:30 pm each day. Failure to do so would have resulted in their homes being torched and burnt down. (223)

In Johannesburg, police managed to disperse a crowd of protesters at Allandale Road near the Castenhof hospital in Midrand. Protesters barricaded roads with burning tires and bottles in Waterfall Extensions 17 and 18. The motive of the protests is still unclear. An eyewitness briefly explained what he could see during the violent protest, 'The protesters are closing both lanes, they are burning tires on both sides. In between the road, they placed bottles to prevent drivers from using the road.' (224)

In Kimberley in the Northern Cape, thousands of community members took to the streets for the third day in a row, bringing the city to a standstill, and vowing not to back down until the mayor suspended the city's Chief Financial Officer and Manager on allegations of corruption. Roads to the city center were blocked, and there were reports that a transformer had been set alight, causing blackouts in most of the city. (225)

In another protest in Johannesburg, police fired rubber bullets to disperse protesters who unashamedly bared their buttocks during a service delivery protest in Diepkloof Soweto. Chris Hani Road was barricaded with rocks and burning tires. (226) 'They [the protesters] were showing their bums by taking their trousers down on the street [to] show their anger with service delivery issues.' Warrant Officer Kay Makhubela said. (227)

Two houses were burnt down and two severely damaged during protests in Coligny, Northwest following the release on bail of two farmers accused of killing a teenager. However, they claimed that they caught him stealing sunflowers and were driving him to the local police station when he jumped off their pickup and broke his neck. It has since been established that the only eyewitness to this supposed crime lied, yet, these men are still in prison. A local auto electrician whose house was burnt down was flabbergasted when the vehicles he was working on, was set alight and burnt out in the process. North West police were on the scene of the violent demonstrations in Coligny, where protesters then set fire to stores. (228)

Footage of the Embalenhle Mall near Sekunda surfaced showing the decrepit aftermath of violence and looting following a protest in June 2018. The South African Police said that vehicles were among some of the property damaged by protesters who were demanding better service delivery. (229)

Plettenberg housing protests turned violent; fires were started all around Plettenberg Bay as petrol bombs were thrown into residential areas. Residents reported the sight as a war zone. Jason Whitehead, a Plettenberg Bay resident who contacted the media, described the protests as 'anarchy' and as 'riots' which are 'out of control.' He said that 'fires being started all over Plett during a gale force heat wave' and 'petrol bombs were being thrown into residential areas.' (230)

In Riebeeck Kasteel in Western Cape, buses filled to capacity by black protestors invaded the town, breaking down, looting and burning everything in sight including wine cellars.

Another warehouse went up in flames in the Kirkwood area where strike action over wages turned violent. (231) (232)

In January 2018, at Overvaal High School in Vereeniging, an Afrikaans high school was swamped by EFF supporters because the school could not admit fifty-five students who insisted on being tutored in English. (233)

Universities were damaged and vandalized by black students in violent protest campaigns known as 'Fees Must Fall.' Minister Nzimande noted at the time that the University of South Africa, Central University of Technology, Durban University of Technology and the University of Fort Hare had their property damaged but had not as yet calculated the cost of damages. (234)

In Vuwani, a town in Vhembe District Municipality in the Limpopo province, a segregation dispute turned violent, and 23 schools were set alight. (235)

Students at the University of KwaZulu-Natal (UKZN) burnt a portion of their law library in a fit of violent wrath. For twenty days, they were protesting for free education and the abolition of annual fee increases. (236)

There is something profoundly wrong in a society where young black people believe that such destruction can result in a restored future. These students are of the impression that they are entitled to free resources because of their 'previously disadvantaged status,' and therefore place no boundaries or limitations on their behavior.

Protesters striking by members of trade union Nehawu have in the past shut down hospitals, not allowing anyone to enter or leave, leaving patients in ICU and various other wards vulnerable. (237)

These protests often lead to looting, property damage, vandalism of stores, barricading of roads and launching petrol bombs into vehicles, as well as throwing rocks at cars and setting buildings alight.

eMbalenhle Mall in Secunda was set alight and torched in June 2018, after looting. This follows a similar scenario, such as when a municipal building and trucks were torched in 2017. (238)

What will be left to fight for as they continue to protest, vandalize and burn down buildings?

Our government remains silent. My president remains unbothered.

Alice VL

DOUBLE STANDARDS, JULIUS MALEMA AND HATE SPEECH IN SOUTH AFRICA

Living in South Africa as a white South African has become much like wearing a target on my back. To black South Africans, it means little to nothing that most white South Africans weren't raised according to apartheid or in segregation. It is simple; I am white, and therefore, I am zealously hated. The message is clear; I am an oppressor, I am a thief, I am a trespasser, and I must be driven from my country or be killed.

South Africa today makes it acceptable for black South Africans to refer to white South Africans as thieves. It is politically acceptable to blame the minority for the incompetencies and failures of this country now, 24 years after the ANC government was inaugurated, following the apartheid era. [239]

We are constantly being threatened by hearing that we should be killed or alternatively, escape back to where we came from. We are subjected to accusations of being responsible for the murder of their forefathers, robbing them of their homes and land, and for continuously spewing racial hatred at them. [240] [241]

Alice VL

Yet, the moment any white South African points out the failures of the ANC and government, we are accused of white-privilege, entitlement and of white supremacy. Apartheid's principal crime was its oppression and segregation laws, yet, right now, Black Economic Empowerment and Affirmative Action are no different. The instant we engage in cultural pride and heritage, white South Africans are once again accused of racial tendencies.

Vicky Momberg, a white South African was found guilty on four counts of crimen injuria in November 2017 for a rant when she vented at a police officer after a smash-and-grab incident in Northriding, Johannesburg in 2016. In a video clip that went viral, she could be heard complaining about the 'caliber of blacks.' The court sentenced her to three years in prison, one year suspended which was in turn, suspended for another three years on condition that she did not commit the same offense again. (242)

The reality in South Africa is that when a white South African insults a black South African, we are harshly punished. When a South African National Defense Force officer made a public statement that 'white people's eyes and tongues must be gorged out,' he was simply reprimanded, and warned not to do it again. (243) Only once the post began gaining footing did

Democratic Alliance Shadow Minister of Defence and Military Veterans, Kobus Marais urgently apply to the Minister of Defence and Military Veterans, Nosiviwe Mapisa-Nqakula for a formal investigation into the officer for hate speech. Following the investigation, he was subsequently dismissed by the South African National Defence Force.

Major Mageti Mohlala, a former member of the South African National Defence Force and in whose dismissal lobby group AfriForum played an instrumental part, said in reaction to a photo of an assaulted 80-year-old man that the attackers 'should have stabbed out his eyes and tongue so that they would have been the last people he ever saw and that he could have gone to his grave with this nightmare.' He went on to say that 'Apartheid is in him. All of these old white people think we are stupid when they say they were opposed to apartheid. We will not forget what they have done. Now it is the white people's turn.' (244)

We are harshly criticized when we point out the failures of the ANC—even though they are not pointed to as a race, but a political party.

Penny Sparrow, an estate agent from KwaZulu-Natal, who referred to black people who littered on a Durban beachfront as monkeys, was fined R150,000 while Velaphi Khumalo, who said that white people in South Africa deserve to be butchered like Jews was simply instructed to issue an apology. (245)

South African social media users have been shocked by the handling of hate-speech posts. Certain users claim that when posts or images are uploaded concerning the current critical farm murders taking place, the social media platform, specifically Facebook, removes these posts and/or disables their accounts.

However, when hate-speech posts are uploaded and subsequently reported, the response by Facebook is disturbing when their response indicates that posts such as hate-speech do not violate their standards. (246) (247)

KILL THE BOER – KILL THE FARMER – THE SONG

Democratic Alliance member of the KwaZulu-Natal legislature, Tom Stokes said that he believed that farm murders are aggravated by Julius Malema's leading and singing of struggle songs that promotes, endorses, and enforces the blatant killing of farmers. (248)

To the majority of white South Africans, Malema's singing of the song 'kill the Boer' while addressing students and followers at rallies is deemed as a call to murder and eradicate the country of its white population. (249)

Tom Stokes' view is supported by Advocate Anton Alberts of the Freedom Front Plus who said, as an influential youth leader, Julius Malema creates an atmosphere in which 'reckless thoughts and actions flourished.' (250)

You don't need to be intellectually challenged to understand that Julius Malema's comments create a willingness and a prod for 'those' who are ready to engage in civil war in an attempt to eradicate white citizens and farmers in South Africa. The ANC defends the singing of these songs and justifies them as merely a preservation of struggle literature.

In 2011, the Equality Court ruled that the words 'shoot

the Boer' amounted to hate speech in a case in which Afrikaner lobby group AfriForum took then ANC Youth League leader Julius Malema to court for chanting the song. (251)

The offensive IsiZulu Struggle song, Kill The Boer, boasts with lyrics such as 'mother gets happy when we kill/hurt/hit the Boer' and 'my father gets happy when we beat the Boers, climb on top of the house and kill them.' 'Kill the settler, kill the Boer, one bullet, one settler' is another popular struggle song that was sung in October 2017 when Black First Land First (BFLF), the ANC Youth League (ANCYL) and the uMkhonto weSizwe Military Veterans Association (MKVA) staged a protest to deliver three different memorandums, 'dealing with the settler colonizer.' (252) (253)

THE RED BERETS

Julius Malema, the man with the red beret who leads the EFF with utter disregard for the law. He is regularly and habitually filmed inciting violence against white South Africans. He publicly declared that our government and laws are not in a position to thwart his plans for land-grabbing and that he answers to no-one, also insisting that South Africa withdraws from Commonwealth.

He demands and insists that all South Africans, regardless of race or ethnicity speak the language of Swahili and that he thereby seeks to erase other languages such as Afrikaans. In another irresponsible outburst, Julius Malema issued a stern warning to the President of the United States of America to 'stay out' of South Africa's domestic affairs. 'Furthermore, we want to send a strong message to the USA authorities, just like we did with the Australian authorities to stay out of South Africa's domestic affairs.' (254)

And again, 'The EFF is in charge – the ANC is following us.' Julius Malema is known to repeatedly spark uproars which results in parliament being overthrown and plunged into chaos.

Alice VL

But, it was when Julius Malema was captured on camera discharging what appeared to be an automatic assault rifle at the Sisa Dukashe Stadium in Mdantsane outside East London, that white South Africans became unnervingly aware of his volatility and 'madness.' (255)

In June 2018, when Julius Malema was asked on Twitter whether he was behind the farm murders, his answer was 'Maybe. Maybe not.' (256)

In Newcastle, Julius Malema blatantly announced that no white person rightfully owns any land in South Africa. He not so subtly hinted at the fact that if the land is not given to black people; they may call for 'slaughter.' Addressing hundreds of EFF supporters, Julius Malema casually said, 'We are not calling for the slaughter of white people, at least for now.' He continued by saying that despite putting pressure on then-president Jacob Zuma to step down, it is the 'monopoly capital' which is the foremost enemy and who continue to benefit from the land while black people continue to struggle. Among his continuous rantings, he said, 'The rightful owners of the land are black people. No white person is a rightful owner of the land here in South Africa or the whole of the African continent.' (257)

Julius Sello Malema was born on 3 March 1981 and is a

member of parliament and leader of the Economic Freedom Fighters, a far-left and racial nationalist South African political party which was founded in 2013. Prior to founding the EFF, he served as president of ANCYL from 2008 to 2012, when he was expelled from the party. He was described by then-president Jacob Zuma as the 'future leader' of South Africa even though he is branded as a 'reckless populist' with the potential to destabilize South Africa while sparking racial tensions and conflict.

Julius Malema was convicted of hate speech by the Equality Court of South Africa. He was fined R50,000 and ordered to apologize unconditionally. In November 2011, he was found guilty of sowing divisions within the ANC and together with his two-year suspended sentence in May 2010, he was suspended from the party for five years. This was following a 2009 incident when he told a group of Cape Town students at a South African Students' Congress (SASCO) meeting that the woman who had accused President Zuma of rape had a 'nice time' with him because in the morning she had 'requested breakfast and taxi money.'

In March 2010, at a rally on a university campus, Julius Malema unashamedly and fearlessly sang 'Ayasab Amagwala' (the cowards are scared). His singing was compared to similar chants by deceased Youth League leader Peter Mokaba which was labeled as hate speech by the South African Human Rights Commission.

On 26 March 2010, the Gauteng High Court ruled that the song (which Julius Malema had continued singing at public gatherings) was 'unconstitutional and unlawful,' and that any person chanting it could face charges of incitement to murder. The song called for the killing of the 'farmer/white man,' yet the ANC defended the song and announced it would appeal the ruling. (258)

In April 2011, lobby group Afriforum brought a case of hate speech against Julius Malema for continuing to sing the song. During his legal battle, Winnie Madikizela-Mandela and Secretary General, Gwede Mantashe firmly supported him. In 2011, Julius Malema was convicted of hate speech after singing 'Dubula iBunu' (Shoot the Boer). (259)

In 2012, Julius Malema was charged with fraud, money-laundering, and racketeering. After numerous postponements, his case was dismissed by the courts in 2015 due to excessive delays by the National Prosecuting Authority, leading to perceptions that the charges were politically motivated. Again in 2018, AfriForum announced that it would seek private prosecution of Julius Malema on corruption charges.

Alice VL

Many black South Africans have turned to social media to blatantly profess their hatred for white South Africans, and their intention to murder the last white person in 'their' country.

David Masotla wrote, 'Next year is the last year for all whites. I MEAN ALL WHITES to apologize for what their granddaddies did to ours. No exceptions. We gave y'all more than 15 years to make it up to us, but some of you are still acting smart. Your racist remarks are counted. Watch out.' (260)

Sabelo Pama wrote, 'This weekend I must kill the devil settler.' (261)

Ahmed El Saud wrote, 'Kill the fucking whites now!!! if you are afraid for them, let's do it for you. In return, you can pay us when the job is done...text us...we are not afraid.' (262)

Mveleli Mogolwani Gwabeni wrote, 'then we must continue to kill more of their farmers at least to make up for what they did to us.' (263)

Mampuru Mampurur wrote, 'We need to unite as black people. There are less than 5 million whites in South Africa vs. 45 million of us. We can kill all this white within two weeks. We have the army and the police. If those that are killing the farmers can do it what are you waiting for? Shoot the Boer, kill the farmer.'

Alice VL

(264)

Karabo Khama wrote, 'Shelly-Anne Parker Loubser your piglets might be born here, but they are not Africans. A pig born in a lion's den does not automatically become a lion. You pink pigs do not belong here. I want you all out of MY ANCESTRAL LAND. Go back to Europe where you come from.' (265)

'Yolanda Ndwandwe wrote, 'Definitely. Domestic workers must be urged to poison their madam's whole family. One white family at a time.' (266)

Velaphi Khumalo, ANC Party Member, wrote, 'I want to cleanse this country of all white people. They deserved to be hacked and killed. You must be skinned alive and your children used as fertilizer.' (267)

Another one from him, 'Noo seriously though u oppressed us when u were a minority and then make u call us monkeys, and we suppose to let it slide. White people in South Africa deserve to be hacked and killed like Jews. U have the same venom moss. Look at Palestine. Noo u must be bushed alive and skinned and your offsprings used as garden fertilizer.' (268)

As a white South African, I, along with the remainder of the minority have reached a stage of helplessness and utter hopelessness after twenty-four years under the ANC rule. We have progressively adapted and possibly yielded into accepting the assaults against us, as well as the destruction of the country that was once home to us all. It has become a new normal to witness the destruction of our cities, the destroying of our universities and schools, the wrecking of our world-class hospitals, roads, and even transportation. We know that by attempting to create awareness of the crimes against us; the brutal farm murders, the corruption and the blatant hatred against white South Africans, we are at risk of being accused of white-driven propaganda. We cringe and scroll past racial hatred and comments on social media and ignore that which reminds us of the fact that we are waiting for our turn to be slaughtered. At any given minute, it could be any white South African's turn.

One of Julius Malema's posts on his social media platform, Twitter caused a tremendous stir on the social media platform. He posted a video of controversial U.S. activist Louis Farrakhan in which he called on black people to use violence against white people to rectify injustices. 'There is no freedom without the shedding of blood; I'm sorry to say this, non-violence is not going to bring the land back to us, our unity will keep us from having to fire a shot.' (269) He goes on to say that white people are always preaching non-violence, but they themselves have used it to get ahead. 'Don't let that white man tell you that

Alice VL

violence is wrong; every damn thing he got, he got it by being violent. He [the white man] is worthy to be hated, worthy because of the evil that he does.' Twitter users had mixed emotions about the video, with some saying that Julius Malema was inciting violence while others were in support of the leader who wears a red beret. (270)

Lwanda Silwana posted a call to Somalians, Zimbabweans, and all other Africans for mass land expropriation without compensation to a social media group called Masiphumelele, a township in Cape Town, South Africa. 'Let's make this day a mass destruction.' Lwanda Silwana asked for the destruction to white property, cars, and government assets until 'we get answers.' (271) (272)

In July 2018, the Black First Land First party was hauled to the Equality Court for a pre-trial conference after they were accused of using hate speech. BFLF leader Andile Mngxitama said in a tweet that the movement was prepared to 'take up arms' to 'protect itself' and suggested the complaint was nothing more than an attempt to 'ban' the party. The Party said, 'White monopoly capital via the SAHRC (South African Human Rights Commission) wants the court to ban BFLF and declare slogans such as 'land or death,' 'by any means necessary' and 'one settler one bullet' as hate speech.'

Alice VL

Andile Mngxitama's tweets include

- One settler one bullet

- One bullet one settle

- If I don't kill a Boer tonight, an Indian will do

- Mngxitama leading from in front. One settler one bullet.

- I have aspirations to kill white people, and this must be achieved.

- The enemy is the white settler elite. Let us direct our anger
  at the real enemies.

- When will we kill them?

- Wind + matches + white-owned farms.

- Take back the land. Land or death.

- We will kill you like you killed my people.

- We must prepare ourselves to meet the colonial settler fact
  to face in 2018 #landordeath

Alice VL

- Long-term solution = kill our colonizers.

- I will tell my kids to punch white kids.

- You are a majority, take back the land. Kill the agents of the enemy if necessary. (273) (274) (275)

A South African choir, consisting of all racial groups, including white children, ended their performance at the 10th World Choir Competition in Pretoria by singing an old 'struggle' song that called for the killing of white people and the seizure of land. The DA Mayor of Pretoria, in a resulting debate on Facebook, indicated that he could see nothing wrong with the song labeled as a traditional Zulu War Song and that people were overreacting. According to reports the song was included in the repertoire at the last minute, and despite the objections of some choir members, the children were forced to sing it.

Shane Dladla, the media spokesperson for the competition organizers said that they regarded the singing of the song 'within the context of freedom of speech and that, as the public hearings regarding expropriation of land are still continuing, the singing of the song cannot be regarded as promoting a particular political line of thought.' The song, Thina Sizwe, is one of the songs regularly sung by both Jacob Zuma and Julius Malema at political rallies of the ANC and the EFF. (276)

CHOIR SONG FREELY TRANSLATED

'Thin' abantu boMkhonto sizimisele

(We the people of Mkhonto are prepared)

Ukuwabulala wona amaBhunu

(To kill the Boers)

Hamba kahle Mkhonto Mkhonto

(Go well Mkhonto/spear)

Mkhonto weSizwe

(Spear of the Nation).

Thina sizwe esimnyama

(We the black the nation)

Sikhalelela izwe lethu

(Are we weeping for our land)

Elathathwa ngabamhlophe

(Which was taken away from us by white people).

Mabayeke umhlaba wethu

(Let them return our land).' (277)

Mseleni Mogolwane Gwabeni, who is a member of the
South African Police Service according to his Facebook profile,

made a statement on his social media platform, 'then we must continue to kill more of their farmers at least to make up for what they did to us.' (278)

Chris Gumotso, who is employed at the South African Police Service Youth Crime Prevention Desk according to his Facebook profile, placed the following statement on Facebook, 'All white man...deserve to die...in future...f*©k u...Mr white man." He also placed photos of firearms on his police desk on his profile with this quote: "I predict the civil war.. in mzansi...by 2019...take out our guns...fighters coz Asijiki.' (279)

Black First Land First made no secret of their hatred and celebrated an attack on an Eshowe farm. 'Black First Land First (BFLF) welcomes the actions of the community. No politician, police or constitution will protect us blacks. We, therefore, have a God-given duty to defend ourselves. Farms, where the murders of black people take place, must be expropriated without compensation by the community. BLF is inspired by the revolutionary actions of the people of Eshowe. If we want freedom, we must charge forward like the brave blacks of Eshowe!' (280)

A case study was conducted privately in social media postings of racial spurs during 2016.

Alice VL

The numbers for white South African racial slurs showed that Penny Sparrow was reported on 4501 times.

Chris Hart was reported on 1155 times.

Justin Van Vuuren was reported on 251 times.

Mabei Jansen was reported on 840 times.

Vicki Momberg 419 times and Matthew Theunissen, 553 times.

The numbers for black South African racial slurs showed that Jacob Zuma was reported on 117 times.

Julius Malema 163 times.

Lulu Xingwane 11 times.

Jonathan Janse was reported on 10 times and Steven Naai

7 times.

Vuyiswa Bhefile KaHlazo was reported on 3 times, Esethu Hasane 40 times.

Velaphi Khumalo 136 times, Tlou Molele 16 times, Luvuyo Menziwa 131 times and Benny Morota, twice.
(281)

Alice VL

Alice VL

THE STOLEN LAND ISSUE IN SOUTH AFRICA

What played out in Parliament in March 2018 was nothing short of momentous and horrifying at the same time. With the newly appointed President Cyril Ramaphosa, the ANC and the Economic Freedom Fighters joined forces and called for the expropriation of land without compensation.

The motion called into question the constitutional reimbursement, triggering celebratory delight on the one side, and distrustful apprehension on the other, as all South Africans revert to disagreeable positions on land and property in South Africa. The motion convened a Constitutional Review Committee and contained varied political parties to review and amend section 25 of the Constitution which would enable the South African government to expropriate land and without compensation to current landowners.

President Cyril Ramaphosa has sworn to restructure land by taking it from white farmers and handing it over to black South Africans.

Alice VL

Only from white farmers.

'Accelerate our land redistribution programme not only to redress a grave historical injustice but also to bring more producers into the agricultural sector and to make more land available for cultivation. We will pursue a comprehensive approach that makes effective use of all the mechanisms at our disposal. Guided by the resolutions of the 54th national conference of the governing party, this approach will include expropriation of land without compensation.' (281)

Gugile Nkwinti - Minister of Water and Sanitation, has stated, 'all land going back to 1652 must be returned to the people. Nobody was asleep when land was taken. It was taken through brutal wars of colonialism.' (282)

Julius Malema – EFF, 'The time for reconciliation is over. Now is the time for justice. We must ensure that we restore the dignity of our people without compensating the criminals who stole our land.' (283)

And then there's the social media opposition by black South Africans to white-owned-land.

Makhwela Lefty Monyela wrote, 'FUCK U ALL WHO THINK HE DESERVE TO DIE JUST BECAUSE OF STEALING A FUCKEN

TRACTOR! There are people here who stole our land n it affected our forefathers, us, our children n our generation to fucken come! That's what we call stealing! Not a fucken stupid tractor. Those that stole our land deserve to die all of them even their kids and their generation to come!' (284)

Andile (@Mngxitama) (BLF), 'Whites are alien in South Africa. How can this historical fact be racism? Whites are colonialists who stole our land.' (285)

Official Wanda Sykes, 'White people don't steal wallets. They steal countries.' (286)

EFF – Jagersfontein, 'It is a known fact that no white man came with land in Azania (South Africa). They came with ships and guns to massacre people, steal land, and enslave black people not only in SA, the whole Africa, but even today white man owns Africa's land and leaves the majority to poverty and starvation. As EFF our conscious is clear, let them bring back our land.' (287)

Article by Gerhard Uys, Farmer's Weekly, November 2017:

A land audit conducted by Agri SA and Agri Development Solutions has provided new figures for land ownership between 1994 and 2017. 'Speaking at the launch of the land audit report,

Dan Kriek, President of Agri SA, said that transactional data had been sourced from the deeds offices to determine the changes in land ownership while additional data had been obtained from Stats SA and the Department of Agriculture, Forestry, and Fisheries, the report said.'

According to Omri an Zyl, Executive Director of Agri SA, from a total surface area of 122 million hectares, 97 million hectares had been available for agriculture in 1994. This figure has since decreased to 93,3 million hectares, due to the growth of mining and industry, and the expansion of urban centers, government land, and privately owned and national conservation areas.

'In 1994, government-owned 13 814 336 hectares, with former homelands, self-governing states, and trusts owning an additional 18 036 773 hectares. Between 1994 and 2016, the government bought 2 208 031 hectares for agricultural development purposes, and 641 267 hectares for urban development. Land reform beneficiaries chose to take compensation, rather than land, for about 2 772 457 hectares,' Van Zyl said.

Between 1994 and 2016, disadvantaged individuals had purchased 4 373 376 hectares for agricultural purposes. During the same period, black owners of agricultural land had sold 388 570 hectares back to white farmers. (288)

If our history lessons are to be believed (the same history that has been removed from our educational system), settlements of Bantu-speaking people were present south of the Limpopo River (now the northern border with Botswana and Zimbabwe) by between the 4th and 5th century.

They displaced, conquered and absorbed the original Khoi-San, the Khoi-Khoi, and San tribes. The Bantu slowly moved south to the now known KwaZulu-Natal Province, believed to date back to around 1050. The southernmost group was known as the Xhosa tribe who reached the Great Fish River, today known as the Eastern Cape Province.

In 1487, the Portuguese explorer Bartolomeu Dias led the first European voyage to land in southern Africa. On 4 December, he landed at Walfisch Bay (now known as Walvis Bay in present-day Namibia). This was south of the furthest point reached in 1485 by his predecessor, the Portuguese navigator Diogo Cão (Cape Cross, north of the bay).

Dias continued down the western coast of southern Africa. After 8 January 1488, prevented by storms from proceeding along the coast, he sailed out of sight of land and passed the southernmost point of Africa without seeing it. He reached as far up the eastern coast of Africa to what he called, Rio do Infante, which is suspected to be the present-day Groot River, in May 1488. But on his return, he discovered the Cape, which he first named Cabo das Tormentas (Cape of Storms).

His King, John II, renamed it Cabo da Boa Esperança, or Cape of Good Hope. Representatives of the British East India Company did call intermittently at the Cape in search of provisions as early as 1601 but later came to favor Ascension Island and St. Helena as choice ports of asylum.

Dutch interest was aroused after 1647 when two employees of the Dutch East India Company (VOC) were shipwrecked there for several months. In 1652, a century and a half after the discovery of the Cape sea route, Jan van Riebeeck established a station at the Cape of Good Hope, which would later become Cape Town, on behalf of the Dutch East India Company.

Some of the earliest mixed-race communities in the country were later formed through unions between vrijburgers, their slaves, and various aboriginal tribes. This led to the development of a new ethnic group, the Cape Coloureds, most of whom adopted the Dutch language and Christian faith.

Alice VL

Vrijburgers who became independent farmers on the frontier were known as Boers, with some adopting semi-nomadic lifestyles being symbolized as trekboers. The Boers formed loose mercenaries, which they termed commandos, and forged alliances with Khoisan groups to deter Xhosa raids. Great Britain occupied Cape Town between 1795 and 1803 to prevent it from falling under the control of the French First Republic, which had invaded low countries.

Despite briefly returning to Dutch rule under the Batavian Republic in 1803, the Cape was once again, occupied by the British in 1806. Following the end of the Napoleonic Wars, it was formally ceded to Great Britain and became an integral part of the British Empire. British immigration to South Africa began around 1818, which culminated in the arrival of the 1820 Settlers. The new settlers were encouraged to settle to increase the European workforce and to reinforce frontier regions against Xhosa infiltrations.

In the first two decades of the 19th century, the Zulu people grew in power and expanded their territory under their leader, Shaka Zulu. His conflict led indirectly to the killing of an estimated 2M people. This resulted in utter devastation and depopulation of the inland in the early 1820's.

Alice VL

Sprouting from the Zulu, the Matabele tribe ended up creating a larger empire which included large parts of the highveld under their king, Mzilikazi. During the early 1800s, many Dutch settlers departed from the Cape Colony, where they had been subjected to British control. They migrated to what was known as Natal, Orange Free State, and Transvaal regions.

The Boers founded the South African Republic and their provinces, now Gauteng, Limpopo, Mpumalanga, the North West Province and the Orange Free State. The discovery of diamonds in 1867 and gold in 1884 gave birth to the mineral revolution and hugely increased economic growth and immigration and at the same time, intensified British efforts to gain control over the native people.

The Anglo-Zulu War was fought in 1879 between the British Empire and the Zulu Kingdom. Following Lord Carnarvon's successful introduction of the federation in Canada, it was surmised that similar political exertions, coupled with military campaigns, might prosper in the kingdoms, tribal areas, and Boer republics in South Africa.

In 1874, Sir Henry Bartle Frere was sent to South Africa as the High Commissioner for the British Empire to put such plans into motion. The Boer Republics successfully resisted British invasions during the First Boer War during the period 1880 to 1881 using guerrilla warfare tactics, which were well suited to South Africa's local conditions.

The British came back with greater numbers, more experience, and a brand-new strategy in the Second Boer War between 1899 and 1902 but suffered heavy casualties. Still, they were ultimately successful. During the Dutch and British colonial years, racial segregation was mostly informal, though legislation was endorsed to control the settlement and movement of native people, including the Native Location Act of 1879.

Barely eight years after the end of the Second Boer War and after tough negotiations which lasted for four years, the British Parliament (South Africa Act 1909) granted nominal independence and created the Union of South Africa on 31 May 1910.

In 1931, the Union of South Africa was fully independent from the United Kingdom. In 1934, the South African Party and the National Party merged to form the United Party – seeking reconciliation between the Afrikaners and the English.

However, in 1939 the party split due to the entry of the union in World War II as a supporter of the United Kingdom. The National Party strongly opposed the entry. On 31 May 1961, the country became a republic following voting in which voters elected in favor of a republic, even though the Natal province was against this.

Queen Elizabeth II was stripped of her title as Queen of South Africa, and the then governor, General Charles Robberts Swart became the Republic of South Africa's state president. The White South African was a new nation, born in Africa. They named Afrikaans as their language and called themselves the Afrikaners; they adopted Africa as their tribal name.

In December 1834, slavery was abolished in the Cape Colony, two years before the start of the Great Trek. Shaka Senzaghakohona of the Zulu nation was born around 1787, over a hundred years after the Europeans arrived in South Africa. He united by force and murdered a number of small tribes in the Zulu nation around 1819.

Our history has been erased from schools and educational institutions in an attempt to erase our heritage and ties to South Africa. (289) (290) (291) (292) (293)

Alice VL

EXPROPRIATION WITHOUT COMPENSATION AND THE FOREIGN INVESTOR

While our president strips white South Africans from owning land, we remain vulnerable as we are faced blatant but permissible theft of our homes. After all, South Africa's population stands at 55.91 million and over 80% of this number is made up of the black population, leaving white South Africans in the minority of an estimated 8%.

What about the foreign investor? The law was controversial right from the start; foreign governments and companies stated that it would reduce their investment-protection in this country and would probably lead to unwillingness to invest in South Africa. After all, the law exposes all foreign investors to equal rules on land expropriation as it does a citizen of South Africa unless the government decides otherwise.

The commencement of the expropriation without compensation law was met with fierce opposition from the Democratic Alliance and saw powerful lobbying by foreign governments and organizations such as the EU Chamber of Commerce and Industry in Southern Africa. The warning was clear, 'It would promote discomfort leading to discouragement related to new investments.'

Even though it was silently and initially unnoticed signed into law by then President Jacob Zuma in 2015, the law was called into force by the publication of president Ramaphosa's commencement notice in February 2018 who had signed the motion a month before.

The law in effect replaces bilateral investment treaties between South Africa and other countries, which includes special protections such as property rights for companies from outside investors. Instead, the new law allows foreign investors the same rights and protections available to their South African peers.

In doing so, it excludes foreign arbitration for dispute. Foreign investors are now constrained to exhaust all domestic and local options available to them before there is a possibility of international arbitration. This, however, is only permittable if the South African government chooses to consent to outside arbitration. This drew immense criticism from American organizations and the Netherlands Government, but recent developments may move the focus to an entirely different aspect of the law.

Under the Protection of Investment Act, 'Investors have the right to property in terms of section 25 of the Constitution.' This clause of the constitution is currently being debated to determine if it should be altered to allow for easier expropriation of land without compensation.

The new law will state that foreign investors should receive no special treatment when government applies decisions 'designed to protect or advance persons, or categories of persons, historically disadvantaged by unfair discrimination on the basis of race, gender or disability.' (294)

Alice VL

ESCALATING POVERTY IN SOUTH AFRICA

We are desperate to contribute to our country's economy while feeding our families. But, as white South Africans, we may not as much as apply for any position that is somehow affiliated with the South African Government. Our privately-owned companies are under pressure to employ candidates under the Black Economic Empowerment law, also known as Broad-Based Black Economic Empowerment.

We are trained in specialized positions, but we may not as much as seek employment within any government sector or affiliation. Yet, daily we are met with employees incapable of performing their duties, or unwilling to perform in the work sector.

It is frustrating. It is devastating and brings with it the inability to support our families or offer them a warm bed to sleep in and in turn, we become weaker. The Afrikaner pride grows weaker. Desperation increases when we are treated as 'nothing.' We don't have the right to work and sustain our families. Managers or recruiters in the public service sectors have

Alice VL

been incentivized to keep white employees out for racial and political reasons, but also, in the name of transformation.

The opinion in the public service sector is that it is far better for South Africa to leave a vacancy unfilled than to employ a white person, despite the requirements of the position, or the white candidate's qualifications. Not only is this policy setting up the selected employees for failure, but in turn, they are failing people of all races who are dependent on the government.

Documents circulated hint that incentives, including bonuses and promotions, are available for keeping white South Africans out of public sector jobs. This places our healthcare at risk since patients of all races are vulnerable when it comes to treatment by untrained, uneducated, and inexperienced staff.

Our schools are at risk, and our children are being failed when unskilled teachers are brought in to provide education at enormously low academical standards.

The result is that all of South Africa grows increasingly vulnerable as South African Police Service and South African Military and Navy recruits are accepted despite failing the standards as set out by the previous government.

Municipal services are compromised, the economy is at

risk, and the way is paved for a whole new sense of entitlement and supremacy by one race.

The affirmative action and black economic empowerment plans are not working. Unqualified staff are employed; their ineptness particularly affects the poor and vulnerable communities. Again, by enforcing these employment laws, and by excluding white South Africans from the job market, the government believes that they are dictating political correctness.

Not only are positions filled based on the grounds of race, but also on political allegiances to the ruling party. Skills are not a prerequisite. Experience, it turns out, is a subordinate criterion. Can there be any question as to why so many government sectors are having problems? Experienced staff with years of service have systematically been denied promotions and encouraged to take early retirement simply because they are of the wrong color. (295) (296) (297) (298)

The intentions of the ANC government in Circular 213-6 is more evident today than ever before. But the devastation is further complicated by the government's lack of accountability. South African politicians are answerable to their party leaders and not to the constituency. Something is wide of the mark when

Alice VL

bad decisions are made, and no action is taken by those responsible for the failure of our health care system, educational institutions, service delivery, our police force, and other public service departments. Most of the problems mainly arise due to their employment criteria. There is a dire skills shortage accompanied by the government's failure to train so-called professionals. The majority of the protests in South Africa come as a result of rage, corruption, discrimination, and the government's total lack of accountability. In suitable job categories, white South Africans are limited to a small percentage of the total workforce in this country. BEE, BEE+, Affirmative Action and anti-white laws have paved the way for a growing number of white South Africans living below the poverty line in South Africa.

Working-class white people, most of them Afrikaans-speaking, are currently undergoing an intense crisis in South Africa as they are refused employment in their own country. Approximately one-third of all white Afrikaners are now financially challenged and living in squatter camps as a direct result of the ANC government's anti-white job laws. (299)

Desperate to undo years of racial inequality, the ruling ANC government introduced laws that encouraged employment for black South Africans only, allowing them the foremost share of the economy. There are currently eighty white squatter townships in the country where families live in dire poverty, with very little food or running water or electricity. Shacks made up of zinc sheets are erected where children spend their days in the often muddy and harsh environments with ditches and filthy pools and no running water. These are the conditions which the employable South Africans and their families are forced to live in with barely enough food to go around.

Following the end of apartheid in 1994, the majority of white South Africans have had little to no compassion from the ANC government who believes that white South Africans profited from the apartheid government. Our president has made it clear that 'our own people must run their business,' and they must be empowered to do just that. 'People are tired of having the businesses in our country being run by a minority. Our own people must run their business, and we will empower them to do that.' Ramaphosa said during the launch of his Thuma Mina campaign in Stanger, Durban. 'The government is working 'feverishly' to ensure that black South Africans become 'serious businesspeople. We want them to run businesses and employ others. We want radical economic empowerment and transformation to be the order of the day,' he said after handing out title deeds in the area. 'The ANC is now involved in a massive project to give our people's dignity back to them by giving title deeds and land. We are committed to this irrevocably. Our people's dignity was rubbished by apartheid rule.'

Title deeds were part of an economic renewal process that would lead to empowerment. 'Our people can empower themselves with assets, including land. We are going to give land to our people; we are just not going to talk about it. We have set up an inter-ministerial committee to look at land renewal and reform. We are going to set up an expert task team that is also doing that. The slogans are over now; we are now going to give land to our people. This is the fulfillment of a promise the ANC made because we are a listening organization.' (300)

SASOL (South African Synthetic Oil Liquid) recently launched a shares-ownership-scheme for their black employees only. (301)

A South African retail giant, Woolworths, has come under fire for advertising positions only open to African, colored and Indian candidates. Woolworths wasted no time in responding on their website, Facebook and Twitter. 'Over the past few days, we've been accused of racist employment practices. We'd like to state the facts: Like all South African companies, Woolworths has a role to play in transformation. For this reason, SOME positions (where there is under-representation) are designated for EE groups. The designated groups are Blacks, Coloreds, Indians, women, and people with disability. As per the Employment Equity Act of 1998, Woolworths is expected, like all SA companies with more than 50 employees, to plan our workforce by race, gender, and disability. Our workforce is diverse and includes people of all races (Black, White, Colored, Indian), gender and disability. (302)

Alice VL

THE LACK OF FORMAL QUALIFICATIONS IN HIGH-UP PLACES

The qualifications of government officials and politicians are regularly brought into question with accusations of falsified qualifications or unsuitably qualified people in top positions. Former communications minister Pallo Jordan has resigned from parliament and apologized to the ANC following accusations that his qualifications were falsified. He claimed to be in possession of a Doctorate Postgraduate degree when in actual fact, he possessed no tertiary qualifications. (303)

But, this isn't unique. For years, we have been faced with an unqualified government, including ex-president Jacob Zuma, who had barely attended school. 'I never went to school, but I educated myself. I'm proud of that.' (304)

South African Broadcasting Corporation (SABC), Chief Operating Officer Hlaudi Motsoeneng was accused of lying about having a matric (high school diploma) when he had not graduated high school at all, while SABC chairwoman Ellen Tshabalala was under fire for claiming false qualifications. As SABC Chairperson, she claimed to be in possession of BCom Postgraduate diploma from the University of South Africa when no qualifications from UNISA could be traced. (305) Unlike Pallo Jordan who stepped down as a Member of Parliament, not much has been done to reprimand or rectify the fraudulent qualifications. On the contrary, Hlaudi Motsoeneng was rewarded by new communications minister Faith Muthambi, who appointed him permanent Chief Operating Officer of the broadcasting company. (306)

While an education and strong qualifications are valued in many organizations, the ANC government has downplayed the importance of educational qualifications. The ANC's Chief Whip in Parliament, Stone Sizani, said that with or without academic qualifications, Pallo Jordan remains a source of pride for the party. He said reports that Pallo Jordan did not have the academic qualifications he claimed was 'nothing more than a publicity gimmick.' Commenting on Hlaudi Motsoeneng lying about having a matric qualification to obtain successful employment at the SABC, a 'law firm' report cleared Hlaudi Motsoeneng of any wrong doing. (307) This is despite the fact that South African Public Protector Thuli Madonsela disclosed that she was in possession of a recording of Hlaudi Motsoeneng saying, 'Yes, I lied. Yes, I put in those symbols.' (308) Ellen Tshabalala's lack of qualifications did not create much of a stir either. In fact, City Press quoted presidency spokesman Mac Maharaj as saying, 'a university degree is no prerequisite for the appointment.' (309) Ellen joined in the qualification debate, saying that SABC employees with university qualifications were doing nothing more than draining their work colleagues. 'Your degrees can't work for you. You need experience to do the work. When these people come with their degrees, they drain the same people [who are skilled but don't have degrees],' He was quoted as saying by the City Press. (310)

The debate surrounding South African president Jacob Zuma's lack of formal education has been a worrying topic of discussion for years. Prince Mashele, CEO of the Forum for Public Dialogue, has been critical of Jacob Zuma's lack of formal education and at the time argued that he was not fit to rule and possessed no formal education. When he attended Marhulana Primary School, he again said that 'I never went to school, but I educated myself. I'm proud of that.'

Our number one employee did not attend school. The same employee tasked with deciding the welfare of a country and in excess of 50-million citizens. The head of South Africa who has the power to decide on business deals, weapons deals, trading, foreign affairs, education, healthcare, welfare, taxes, transportation, aviation, military, only to name a few. 'I never went to school ...'

Alice VL

NELSON MANDELA
President of South Africa
1994 to 1999

Just like the rest of the world, I was seduced by the larger-than-life Mr. Nelson Mandela, and sat glued to the television set the day he took his long walk to freedom with the ever-devoted Winnie Mandela firmly by his side.

I was in awe of the man who had spent twenty-seven long years in prison for nothing more than his relentless pursuit of freedom. *Or so I thought*. I thought that freeing the man who fought for equality and an end to apartheid was a victory for all South Africans, despite the older generation's claims that he was a terrorist who not only acted out against white South Africans but was the mastermind behind acts of violence against his own people.

I listened in awe to his very first speech. I was proud of him and proud of our government for integrating all races.

Alice VL

Nelson Mandela spoke of peace, forgiveness, and of a dream in which he envisioned a Rainbow Nation. But, as the years have progressed, and upon learning of the circular dated back to 1993, I was devastated by the true motives of the ANC government which Nelson Mandela founded.

So, I began to consider the real Nelson Mandela for a moment, while the blissfully ignorant applauded his life as his 100th birthday was celebrated recently. We have all heard the rumors. We've heard the whispers of the older generation, but it was discarded and ignored over the years because Nelson Mandela's promises of a Rainbow Nation would bring with it unity. So, we rebuffed and rejected the warnings.

The truth is that Nelson Mandela pleaded guilty to 156 counts of public violence, including mobilizing terrorist bombing campaigns which resulted in the planting of bombs in public places. Many innocent lives, including those of women and children, were lost as a direct result of Nelson Mandela and his MK (uMkhonto we Sizwe, meaning Spear of the Nation) terrorists. I was horrified to discover his charge list of crimes throughout the years.

Nelson Mandela's Acts of Terrorism

Alice VL

• One count under the South African Suppression of Communism Act No. 44 of 1950, charging that the accused committed acts calculated to further the achievement of the objective of communism;

• One count of contravening the South African Criminal Law Act (1953), which prohibits any person from soliciting or receiving any money or articles for the purpose of achieving organized defiance of laws and country; and

• Two counts of sabotage, committing or aiding or procuring the commission of the following acts:

1) The further recruitment of persons for instruction and training, both within and outside the Republic of South Africa, in:

(a) the preparation, manufacture and use of explosives—for the purpose of committing acts of violence and destruction in the aforesaid Republic, (the preparation and manufacture of explosives, according to evidence submitted, included 210,000 hand grenades, 48,000 anti-personnel mines, 1,500-time devices, 144 tons of ammonium nitrate, 21.6 tons of aluminum powder and a ton of black powder);

Alice VL

(b) the art of warfare, including guerrilla warfare, and military training generally for the purpose of the aforesaid Republic;

(ii) Further acts of violence and destruction, (this includes 193 counts of terrorism committed between 1961 and 1963);

(iii) Acts of guerrilla warfare in the aforesaid Republic;

(iv) Acts of assistance to military units of foreign countries when involving the aforesaid Republic;

(v) Acts of participation in a violent revolution in the aforesaid Republic, whereby the accused injured, damaged, destroyed, rendered useless or unserviceable, put out of action, obstructed, with or endangered:

(a) the health or safety of the public;

(b) the maintenance of law and order;

(c) the supply and distribution of light, power or fuel;

Alice VL

(d) postal, telephone or telegraph installations;

(e) the free movement of traffic on land; and

(f) the property, movable or immovable, of other persons or of the state.

Source: The State v. Nelson Mandela et al., Supreme Court of South Africa, Transvaal Provincial Division, 1963-1964, Indictment.

As a result of these charges, he was given a life sentence in prison of which he served no more than twenty-seven years, during which he gained support as a so-called freedom fighter and black activist, allowing him to walk out and become president four years after his release.

He then systematically went on to release criminals, murderers, and rapists from prison each year, unleashing even more violence, chaos, and death on the people of South Africa.

Over 100,000 people were murdered under Mandela's presidency – an average of 25,000 people each year. (311) (312)

WARFARE AGAINST SOUTH AFRICA

uMkhonto weSizwe was the armed wing of the ANC which was co-founded by Nelson Mandela. Its mission was to fight and engage in warfare against the South African government.

On April 5th, 1980, a unit of MK (Umkhonto we Sizwe) guerrillas attacked the Booysens police station with hand grenades, AK-47 assault rifles and a BPG-7 rocket launcher (bazooka).

On June 1st, 1980, members of MK planted bombs and landmines and sabotaged three of South Africa's leading oil refinery stations, SASOL I and II and NATREF. The bombs exploded almost simultaneously and caused damage of about R6M.

On August 1st, 1980 Det. Sgt. T.G. Zondi escaped death by centimeters when he was fired at with an AK-47 rifle near Sobantu Village in Pietermaritzburg. Empty cartridge casings were found by police near the scene of the shooting, but no-one was arrested despite a massive search for the attackers.

On October 30th, 1980, MK fighters hurled hand grenades at the West Hand Administration Board offices in Diepkloof. Extensive damage was done to the building.

November 21st, 1980, ANC soldier, Gordon Dikebu, fought against the police who had staged a massive early morning raid at his home in Chiawelo. The shoot-out lasted for approximately ten minutes, and an undisclosed number of police were either killed or injured.

On January 16th, 1981, an explosive charge blew up a Mdantsane railway line.

12th April 1981, ANC guerrillas sabotaged a railway line, 15 meters in length at the Vryheid-Richards Bay line. When the locomotive's front detonated the explosive, five trucks were derailed, and the remainder was seriously damaged.

20th April 1981, an electricity supply sub-station in Durban was sabotaged with several limpet mines by a unit of MK soldiers. The blast disrupted telephone communications, closed factories in and around Durban and left thousands of other industrial areas without power. Two transformers at the power station were completely destroyed.

On May 10th, 1981, a hand grenade was thrown at railway policemen killing one of them. The incident took place when the policemen attempted to arrest a man who took out a hand grenade and tried to toss it into their car.

On May 19th, 1981, the railway line linking Port Elizabeth to Johannesburg and Cape Town was blasted by a bomb between Swartkops and New Brighton. The sabotaged railway line was only discovered three hours later when a coach of a Uitenhage train was derailed.

On May 25th 1981, the Fort Jackson police station in East London came under fire with automatic weapons and hand grenade explosions. The unit of ANC guerrillas involved in the attack retreated and was unchallenged.

On May, 27th 1981, a recruiting office of the South African Defense Force near the center of Durban was bombed. Damage was estimated at hundreds of thousands of rands.

On June, 11th 1981, a bomb blasted the Durban Qnpangeni railway line. It was suspected to have been placed on the line and detonated when the train went over it.

On June 26th 1981, a war memorial in Durban was blasted by a bomb in the early hours of the morning. The suspected sabotage operation took place on the day in which the Minister of Transport, Chris Heunis was to meet with leaders of color.

In July 1981, on the 21st, two major power stations in the then Eastern Transvaal were extensively damaged in a sabotage operation by ANC fighters. The explosions were reported to have occurred within an interval of ten minutes apart. The Anort power station, east of Emerlo was blasted at approximately 1:40 am when three explosive charges destroyed as many transformers. A short ten minutes later, two limpet mines destroyed two transformers and five generator couplings at the Camden power station, east of Middleburg.

Then on July 1st, Delmas Power Station near Pretoria was blasted by bombs placed by Umkhonto guerrillas.

On the 26th July 1981, two bombs exploded in a Durban motor-town area of Smith street twenty minutes apart, ripping open show-room frontages of McCarthy Le'yland, damaging four new cars and shattering more than 50 windows on both sides of the street.

7th August 1981 was when an armed battle took place between the police and a unit of MK guerrillas at a road-block set up in Elliot, less than a hundred kilometers from Umtata. Two policemen were killed in the battle.

On the 13th August 1981, Umkhonto soldiers surrounded the headquarters of the South African Defence Force (SADF) complex, the Voortrekkerhoogte military base. Four 122 mm rockets were fired at four strategic points.

September 3rd, 1981, a Mapopane police station in

Pretoria was attacked by ANC guerrillas armed with AK-47 rifles and hand-grenades. Three policemen were killed and several others wounded.

On the 12th September 1981 at 8:45 am, a goods train detonated a landmine at Delville, Wood near Pietermaritzburg cutting the railway line.

October 10th 1981, saw another powerful bomb explode in the center of Durban, destroying a number of buildings. The bomb destroyed part of the local offices of the Department of Co-operation and Development.

On the 11th October 1981, a bomb blast partly-destroyed the Kwa-Zulu government offices near Empangeni. The explosion took place at the superintendent's office.

21st October 1981 again, Umkhonto militants sabotaged five transformers at an Evander electricity sub-station. The explosion took place at 8:45 pm and occurred at the town's main substation causing a blackout for several hours.

23rd October 1981, several transformers were destroyed by ANC patriots at an electricity power station in Witbank. The blast took place at 8:45 pm in Witbank's industrial township.

October 27th, 1981, armed fighters of MK attacked the

Sibasa police station in Northern Transvaal, and two policemen were killed. The guerrillas used hand-grenades, AK-47 automatic rifles, and an RPG-7 rocket launcher.

12th November 1981, four transformers were destroyed at an electric power station in Pretoria North.

I can so clearly remember the late afternoon bombing in May 1983 when a bomb exploded in Church Street, Pretoria. Among the victims was an Air Force soldier; young, unmarried and committed to serving his country. One who wanted nothing more than the safety and security of the people of South Africa. A man about to embark on his journey as an adult, but whose two legs were blown off due to the severity of the blast. For him, his dedication and love for his country died within moments of the attack. He could never again serve as a soldier for his country; his beloved South Africa.   What this soldier couldn't quite fathom was why he was included in the 217 others that were injured and the 19 that died, when he had dedicated his life to serving his country. He would never run on to a training field again; he would never march in a procession, and he would never walk down the aisle or someday, walk his daughter down the aisle.

At the time of the attack, the MK special operations unit

reported to Joe Slovo as chief of staff, and the Church Street attack was authorized by Oliver Tambo.

The Truth and Reconciliation Commission found that the number of civilians versus military personnel killed was unclear. South African Police statistics indicated that seven members of the South African Air Force were killed, and that at least eighty-four of the injured were South African Air Force members or employees. Amnesty was granted by the Truth and Reconciliation Commission in 2000.

On 12th July 1984, a car bomb exploded in Durban, killing five and injuring twenty-seven people. This car bombing was known as the "Jacobs" car bomb, according to an application for amnesty from the Truth and Reconciliation Commission (TRC) by Rayman Lalla, a member of the African National Congress (ANC) and a senior officer in Umkhonto we Sizwe (MK).

Between 1985 and 1987, there were at least 150 landmines on farm roads which killed a total of 125.

In 1985, an Amazimbtoti shopping center bomb killed five people including three children. One of the victims, 5-year-old Isabella Van Wyk, survived, but her 2-year-old brother Arie didn't. Other fatalities included Johannes Smit, 8 years old, Irma Bencini who was 48 years old, and Anna Shearer, 43 years old.

Alice VL

The 60kg bomb planted by MK operative Robert McBride in a car parked outside 'Magoo's Bar' and the adjacent 'Why Not Bar,' went off just after 9 pm on June 14, 1986, killing Angelique Pattenden, Julie van der Linde, and Marchelle Gerrard, while injuring another 73 people. It may be three decades later, but the memories of the devastating bombing on the Durban beachfront is still as fresh in the minds of those affected today as it was thirty-two years ago.

The Johannesburg Magistrate's Court Bombing took place on the 20th May 1987 in Johannesburg, in Gauteng. The massacre, in which three members of the police died, and a further fifteen civilians were injured, was notable to the MK due to the loss of life. It started with a limpet mine attack, followed by a car bomb half an hour later.

On July 30th, 1987, a car bomb was discharged outside the headquarters of Witwatersrand Command Army Base in Quartz Street, Johannesburg. The bombing was executed by Heinrich Grosskopf, under direct orders from the ANC. The explosion was strategically planned to go off at 9:45 am when the morning rush-hour was over, children would be in school and restaurants around the site were still closed. 68 were injured in the bombing while there was one fatality.

Alice VL

On June 23rd, 1988, a Johannesburg Video Arcade bombing killed an unborn child and wounded ten, six of which were black South Africans, three from an Indian family and one white person.

In June 1988, a bomb hidden in a garbage can exploded on a busy street corner outside a Roodepoort Bank, killing three black men and a white woman, and wounding another nineteen people.

At around the same time in 1988, two bombs were detonated at the Pretoria Police Housing Unit, killing four people and wounding another eighteen.

1988 was also the year that a bombing at a Magistrate's Court killed three people.

A bomb explosion affected 57 patrons of a fast-food restaurant in July 1988 in a Johannesburg suburb. This was seen as the latest in a progressive series of attacks aimed at white civilians. The bomb hit a Wimpy Bar restaurant at the Benoni Plaza Shopping Center minutes before noon on one of the busiest shopping days of the week, killing one person and wounding another 56.

Still, in 1988, a car bomb exploded outside a Witbank

Shopping Center, killing two black men and wounding another nineteen. The remainder of the wounded, which totaled forty-two, were white civilians. The attack was consistent with the ANC's bombing campaign that was on-going and targeted.

On the 2nd July 1988, Lester Dumakude, commander of an Umkhonto we Sizwe special operations unit, detonated a car bomb by remote control outside our Ellis Park Rugby Stadium in Johannesburg. The explosion took place minutes after a Free State vs. Transvaal rugby game. Two spectators were killed in the blast, and an additional thirty-seven civilians were injured. Lester Dumakude later testified that the bombing was intended to send a message to the white community and that the rugby stadium was chosen as it was a predominantly white area.

Way back in 1961, Nelson Mandela separated from the African National Congress and created a terrorist wing in retaliation for the ANC's call of non-violence. He later pleaded guilty in court to acts of public violence, but from his prison cell, Nelson Mandela continued to sanction violent crimes, including the wave of bombings which killed and wounded hundreds of civilians. (313)

For all that opposed Nelson Mandela, his wife at the time, Winnie Mandela, advocated 'necklacing,' as opposed to

Mandela's suggestion of cutting off 'the opposition's' noses. Winnie Mandela strongly pursued necklacing; the act of placing a tire around someone's neck, chest, and arms, dousing them with gasoline and setting them alight. Victims take up to twenty minutes to die, suffering severe burns in the process. The fire would continue to burn long after the victim had died, charring the body beyond recognition. (314)

For as long as I am alive, I will never forget the June 1986 death of a South-African woman named Maki Skosana who was burned to death on television as the world watched in utter horror. Anti-apartheid activists wrapped her up in a car tire, doused her with gasoline, and without any hesitation, set her on fire. A new kind of psychological torture was born, not only in the opposing black community but for every white South African. (315)

These acts of torture were reserved for their own people who were branded traitors to the black community. I was horrified when I first learned of necklacing. The images left me reeling, sad, and angry all at the same time. The brutality and cruelty of such a death I would not wish upon my worst enemy.

Nelson Mandela argued that the apartheid regime left him with no option but to fight violence with violence. So, it came as no surprise to discover his support of other leaders enforcing

Alice VL

violence. He maintained close ties to Cuban dictator Fidel Castro and backed Palestinian terrorist leader Yasser Arafat. As president in 1997, he offered South Africa's highest award for a foreigner to Libya's dictator, Colonel Muammar Gaddafi, who had donated $10 million to the ANC. The same award was presented to the corrupt Indonesian president Suharto, whom he said had donated $60 million to the ANC. (316)

His refusal to publicly condemn the hanging of activist Ken Saro-Wiwa in 1995 was seen as a silent nod if approval to Nigerian coup leader Sani Abacha, after his so-called pleadings with the Nigerian leader to excuse Saro-Wiwa. Ken Saro-Wiwa was a Nigerian writer, television producer, and environmental activist. He was also the winner of the Right Livelihood Award and the Goldman Environmental Prize. Ken was a member of the Ogoni people who were part of an ethnic group in Nigeria and whose homeland, Ogoniland had been targeted for crude oil removal since the 1950's.

As president of the Movement for the Survival of the Ogoni People (MOSOP), Ken led a non-violent campaign against environmental degradation of the land and waters of Ogoniland specifically pointing out the Royal Dutch Shell Company. In addition, he was an outspoken critic of the Nigerian Government, who he viewed as unenthusiastic to enforce environmental regulations on foreign petroleum companies operating in the area. At the peak of his campaign, he was tried by a special military tribunal for masterminding the grisly murder of Ogoni chiefs at a pro-government meeting. He was hanged in 1995 by the military dictatorship of General Sani Abacha. (317)

Nelson Mandela was born on July 18, 1918, into a royal family of the Xhosa-speaking Thembu tribe in the South African village of Mvezo, where his father, Gadla Henry Mphakanyiswa served as chief. His mother, Nosekeni Fanny, was the third of his father's four wives, who in total, bore him nine daughters and four sons. After his father died in 1927, 9-year-old Nelson, known by his birth name, Rolihlahla, was adopted by Jongintaba Dalindyebo, who began grooming him for a leadership role within the tribe.

He was the first in his family to receive a formal education and completed his primary school studies at a local missionary school. His teacher nicknamed him Nelson thereby giving him an English name. In 1939, Nelson Mandela enrolled at the University of Fort Hare, the only Western-style higher learning institute for black South Africans at the time. The following year, he and Oliver Tambo were sent home for participating in a boycott against university policies.

When he heard that his guardian had arranged a marriage for him, he fled to Johannesburg and began working as a night watchman and later, as a law clerk where he completed his bachelor's degree part-time. In 1944, he joined the ANC where he and Oliver Tambo established the ANCYL (African National Congress Youth League). He married Evelyn Ntoko Mase shortly after and had four children with her before they divorced in 1957.

Nelson Mandela's devotion to the ANC intensified after the 1948 election victory of the National Party, especially when it introduced an official system of racial classification and segregation or, apartheid. A year later, the ANC implemented the ANCYL's plan to achieve full citizenship for all South Africans through boycotts, strikes and civil disobedience. In December 1956, he and 155 activists were arrested and went on trial for treason. They were all acquitted in 1961, but clashes within the ANC escalated. As a result, a militant faction formed the PAC. (318)

The previous year, police opened fire on black protesters in Sharpeville, killing 69 people. Today it is known as the 'youth killings.' As terror, anger, and riots swept through the country in the aftermath, the South African government banned both the ANC and the PAC. (319)

Alice VL

In 1961, Nelson Mandela co-founded and became the first leader of Umkhonto we Sizwe - 'Spear of the Nation,' a new armed wing of the ANC. Several years later, during the trial that would put him behind bars, he described the reasoning for the radical departure from his party's original doctrine. 'It would be wrong and unrealistic for African leaders to continue preaching peace and non-violence at a time when the government met our peaceful demands with force. It was only when all else had failed, when all channels of peaceful protest had been barred to us, that the decision was made to embark on violent forms of political struggle.' (320)

Under his leadership, MK launched a sabotage campaign against the government, which had only recently declared South Africa a republic that had withdrawn from the British Commonwealth. In January 1962, he traveled illegally to attend a conference of African nationalist leaders in Ethiopia and then to receive guerrilla training in Algeria.

When a group of MK leaders debating a guerrilla rebellion were arrested, evidence was found implicating Nelson Mandela and other members who were brought to trial for sabotage, treason, and conspiracy. (321)

Nelson Mandela went on to earn his Bachelor of Law

degree from the University of London while in prison, and served as a mentor to his fellow prisoners. During his incarceration, he smuggled out what would later become his autobiography, 'Long Walk to Freedom' which was published five years after his release, together with numerous political statements. (322)

Nelson Mandela., the man who won the Nobel Peace Prize received the Presidential Medal of Freedom and the Lenin Peace Prize. The man celebrated by the entire world for his efforts in uniting a country by declaring peace through promises of a Rainbow Nation, and a peaceful future for all South Africans and at the same time, portrayed him as a saint.

But, why does this matter now? Mandela began a series of events which continues to lead our country down a path towards economic devastation, crime, violence, and genocide. The genocide campaign isn't new. It began several years ago even though white South Africans were not yet openly and publicly slaughtered.

Nelson Mandela, the man who declared peace but sang ANC and MK 'struggle' songs about murdering white citizens, alongside his peers. So, with fires raging on, violence that is ignored and chaos all around us in South Africa, it's hard to ignore that the ANC and its leaders, along with the EFF, the BFLF are continuously pouring gasoline onto our already burning fires.

'With our boxes of matches and our necklaces, we shall liberate this country.' – Winnie Mandela.

When documents in Nelson Mandela's handwriting were introduced into evidence at the Rivonia Trial which took place between 1963 and 1964, and which later imprisoned him, the message was clear that 'traitors and informers should be ruthlessly eliminated by cutting off their noses.' He did not deny the validity of these documents, but claimed they were notes jotted down for study materials. (323) (324)

Alice VL

WINNIE MADIKIZELA MANDELA

(ANC Political Activist and ex-wife of Nelson Mandela, Deputy Minister of Arts and Culture, President of ANCWL, member of the NEC of the ANC)

The name Winnie Madikizela Mandela does nothing more than send shivers down my spine. Devoted to her husband Nelson Mandela, she stood closely beside him when he walked out of prison, a free man.

Winnie Mandela was born Nomzamo Winifred Zaniwe Madikizela and was the fifth child of nine children born in Transkei on 26 September 1936. While growing up, her father, Columbus, served as a history teacher but later, he became minister of the Transkei Forestry and Agricultural Department. Winnie's mother known as Gertrude served as a science teacher. Winnie was twenty-two years old when she met Nelson, thirty-eight at the time and who was already a prominent anti-apartheid figure; already a defendant in the Rivonia trail which had begun the year before. (325)

Alice VL

Necklacing was used by the black community to enforce punishment against members who were thought to be traitors collaborating with the apartheid government. In 1986, Winnie Mandela, then-wife of the imprisoned Nelson Mandela stated, 'With our boxes of matches and our necklaces, we shall liberate this country,' was widely seen as an explicit endorsement of necklacing. At the time, it caused the ANC to distance itself from her, although she later took on a number of official positions within the party.

She later denied that she had said this, but a number of journalists heard her and reported her 'quote' around the world. Helen Suzman, who was a close friend of Winnie Mandela, described it as 'reckless and highly irresponsible.' (326)

A thick veil of murkiness continues to engulf the truth around what the events surrounding James Stompei Seipei in 1988; the 14-year-old child who was kidnapped and brutally murdered by the Mandela United Football Club (MUFC), with Winnie herself directly implicated. At the Truth and Reconciliation hearing, the 14-year-old was said to have gone missing from his home before he was beaten and ultimately murdered with a pair of gardening shears. During the hearing, it emerged that Stompie and three other missing boys, Gabriel Mekgwe, Thabiso Mono and Kenneth Kgase, were in the company of MUFC members prior to his disappearance and subsequent murder. Stompie's body was discovered on the outskirts of Soweto on January 4, 1988.

A doctor who initially treated Stompie, Dr. Asvat, was murdered by two young men who posed as patients. The murders of Stompie and Dr. Asvat dominated media attention when The Sunday Star broke the news. With Cyril Mbatha and Nicholas Dlamini convicted of Dr. Asvat's murder, The Sunday Star reported that Winnie may have been involved in Stompie's beating and death. When her name was swiftly removed from The Sunday Star's front pages, many believed it to be as a result of political forces that were plotting to free South Africa's legendary prisoner, Nelson Mandela. Winnie was cleared of Stompie's murder but was sentenced to five years in prison on four counts of kidnapping. She was sentenced to an additional year as an accessory to the assault.

When she appealed, she was ordered to serve a two-year suspended sentence and pay a R15 000 fine. In 1992, Nelson Mandela announced his separation from Winnie Mandela, but said that, 'She endured the persecutions heaped upon her by the government with exemplary fortitude and never wavered from her commitment to the struggle for freedom.' (327)

Alice VL

A year later, she became Deputy Minister of Arts and Culture under Nelson Mandela's presidency, but later, she was dismissed for insubordination. In 1993, Winnie Mandela was elected as the president of the ANC Women's League.

In 1997, Jerry Richardson who served as Winnie's bodyguard in the 1980's and who was a close friend of hers, finally revealed Winnie's role in the killing of Stompie Sepei. 'My hands are full of blood today because I would be instructed to kill, and I would do like I was told.' He told South Africa's Truth and Reconciliation Commission.

At the time of his confession, he was serving a life sentence for the murder of 14-year-old Stompie and recalled beating, torturing and killing people whenever 'mommy' (referring to Winnie Mandela) ordered him to do so. He was adamant that he only beat and killed people under specific orders from Winnie Mandela and participated in a total of four murders ordered by her. (328)

By the time the Truth and Reconciliation Commission was established in 1996, there were accusations against Winnie to justify an in-camera hearing by the Human Rights Violations Committee. In 1997, she was implicated in a number of assaults and murders carried out by the MUFC. Archbishop Desmond

Tutu, Chairman of the Committee, implored Winnie to own up to her intentions in the 1980's and admit that 'things went wrong.' Winnie then admitted that 'things went horribly wrong' and apologized to the families of Stompie Seipei and Dr. Asvat. (329)

Alice VL

THABO MBEKI
President
1999 to 2008

Thabo Mvuyelwa Mbeki, who served as president of South Africa from June 1999 to September 2008, was born on 18 June 1942. In September 2008, with less than a year left in his second term of presidency, he announced his resignation after he was recalled by the National Executive Committee of the ANC. Judge C.R. Nicholson found improper interference in the National Prosecuting Authority (NPA), which included the prosecution of Jacob Zuma for corruption.

However, in January 2009, the Supreme Court of Appeal unanimously overturned Judge Nicholson's verdict, but Thabo Mbeki's resignation held up. (330)

Thabo Mbeki on Zimbabwe, 'The point really about all this from our perspective has been that the critical role we should play is to assist the Zimbabweans to find each other, really to agree among themselves about the political, economic, social, other solutions that their country needs. We could have stepped aside from that task and then shouted, and that would be the end of our contribution. They would shout back at us, and that would be the end of the story. I'm actually the only head of a government that I know anywhere in the world who has actually gone to Zimbabwe and spoken publicly very critically of the things that they are doing.' (331)

In 2004, President Mbeki criticized reporters who argued that crime was out of control in South Africa. He lashed out at them and branded them white racists who want to see the country fail. He said that crime numbers were declining but that journalists had engaged in a campaign to distort reality by describing black people as 'barbaric savages' who 'liked' to rape and kill.

On the ANC's website, president Mbeki berated the pessimists, and although he did not refer to journalist Charlene Smith by name, he referred to an article in which she claimed that South Africa had the highest rate rape in the world and mockingly referred to her as an 'internationally recognized expert on sexual violence.' Since documenting her own rape, she has been actively involved in campaigning for victims of violent sexual offenses. 'She was saying our cultures, traditions, and religions as Africans inherently make every African man a potential rapist, a view which defines the African people as barbaric savages.'

Alice VL

Thabo Mbeki described the newspaper, The Citizen, and reporters who challenged the supposed decline in crime, as cynics who did not trust black rule. (332)

When Jacob Zuma was caught up in a corruption scandal in 2005, Thabo Mbeki removed him from his position as deputy president of South Africa. In addition, Jacob Zuma was facing new rape charges which caused a visible divide between his supporters and Thabo Mbeki's allies in the ANC.

Alice VL

JACOB GEDLEYIHLEKISA ZUMA
President
2009 to 2018

Born on 12 April 1942, Jacob Zuma served as president of South Africa until he stepped down in February 2018. He began engaging in politics when he joined the ANC in 1959. He was an active member of Umkhonto we Sizwe in 1962 and was arrested along with a group of 45 recruits. Jacob Zuma was convicted of conspiring to overthrow the apartheid government and sentenced to ten years in prison which he served on Robben Island with Nelson Mandela and other ANC leaders who were imprisoned during this time.

He initially served as Deputy President of South African between 1999 and 2005, but when his financial adviser, Schabir Shaik was convicted of soliciting a bribe on his behalf, he was summarily relieved of his post. Despite his corruption and rape scandals, Jacob Zuma was elected President of the ANC in December 2007 and president of South Africa in 2009. He was re-elected as ANC leader at an ANC conference in December 2012 where he defeated his challenger, Kgalema Motlanthe and remained in his position as president of South Africa after the 2014 general election. (333)

Jacob Zuma faced momentous legal challenges before and during his presidency, most significantly when he was charged with rape in 2005, even though he was later acquitted. Jacob Zuma was formally charged with raping a 31-year-old woman at his home, the daughter of a struggle comrade and prominent ANC family who was an AIDS activist and known to be HIV positive. Jacob Zuma denied the charges against him and claimed that sex between them was consensual. Throughout the rape trial, Jacob Zuma chanted the song Lethu Mshini Wami (Bring me my machine gun) along with his crowd of supporters which included the ANC Youth League and Communist Party Youth League spokespersons. It made way for enormous political debates when Jacob Zuma, who was head of the National AIDS Council at the time, conceded to the fact that he had not used a condom when he engaged in sexual deeds with the woman who had accused him of rape, despite knowing that she was HIV positive.

In court, he said that he took a shower after having sex with her to 'cut the risk of contracting HIV.' Naturally, his statement was condemned by the judge, health experts, and AIDS activists. In May 2006, he was acquitted of rape when the court established that sex between them was consensual. However, the judge berated him for having unprotected sex with an HIV positive woman who was not his partner. She died in 2016. (334)

He fought allegations of racketeering and corruption which resulted directly from Schabir Shaik's conviction of corruption and fraud. In April 2009, the National Prosecuting Authority dropped the charges against Jacob Zuma and cited 'political interference.' The decision was fiercely challenged by opposition parties, and as at February 2018, the charges were successfully reinstated and are before NPA.

When South Africa's Public Protector revealed that Jacob Zuma had benefited improperly from the extensive state-funded upgrades to his Nkandla home, the Constitutional Court of South Africa unanimously delivered that he had failed to uphold the country's constitution and called for his resignation which led to a failed impeachment attempt in the National Assembly.

President Zuma's tenet as president is estimated to have cost the South African economy R1-trillion (approximately $83-billion). He was further implicated in reports of state capture through his close ties with the Gupta family, and survived multiple motions of no confidence in parliament and within the

ANC.

In December 2017, Cyril Ramaphosa succeeded Jacob Zuma as president of the ANC, and when the ANC 'recalled' Jacob Zuma as president of South Africa, he was under increasing pressure to resign. Facing a motion of no-confidence in parliament, he eventually announced his resignation in February 2018. The National Director of Public Prosecutions at the time, Bulelani Ngcuka, investigated both Jacob Zuma and Chief Whip of the ANC, Tony Yengeni after allegations of abuse of power were brought against them.

In addition, this led to concerns of inappropriate influence in the highly controversial arms deal which questioned the financial benefits to both Jacob Zuma and Tony Yengeni. Tony Yengeni was subsequently found guilty, but the case against Jacob Zuma was dropped. Jacob Zuma's close and corrupt relationship with the Gupta family has been a major source of displeasure within both the ANC, and the South African public.

South African opposition parties made claims of 'State Capture' following accusations by Deputy Finance Minister Mcebisi Jonas and former MP, Vytjie Mentor who exposed that they were offered positions in the cabinet by the Gupta family. The Guptas, known to be close to Jacob Zuma, his family, and other ANC leaders, had inserted themselves into positions where they could offer cabinet positions, and influence decisions of the South African government. (335)

In 2010, Jacob Zuma's bodyguards were implicated in multiple incidents involving members of the public and journalists. A Cape Town student, Chumani Maxwele, was held by police after showing Jacob Zuma's procession a finger gesture. An active ANC member, Chuman Maxwele was released a day later, after submitting a written apology to the police. He later claimed that he was coerced into doing so. He also said that his home had been raided by policemen who were undercover and that he was forced into a vehicle at gunpoint. (336) Journalist Tshepo Lesole was forced to delete photographs of Jacob Zuma's convoy from his camera by police when two photographers were detained by police following photographs they shot of Jacob Zuma's home in Johannesburg. (337)

Sky News reporter Emma Hurd claimed that she had been pushed, shoved and groped by Jacob Zuma's bodyguards in 2009. (338)

During the ANC Centennail celebrations in 2012, Jacob Zuma sang the song 'Dubul' iBhunu' (shoot the boer) after giving a speech. Again, the song is highly contentious as referring to

'Boer' refers to both farmers and the Afrikaner nation of South Africa, who have been beleaguered by violent and brutal farm attacks. (339)

The use of public funds of over R246M was used to 'improve' Jacob Zuma's compound and private residence, Nkandla situated in KwaZulu-Natal. Jacob Zuma eventually apologized for using public money to finance Nkandla, and in April 2016, prominent public figures asked him to resign in light of the scandal mockingly known as 'Nkandlagate.' The village or compound is situated on land owned by the Ingonyama Trust, the legal entity that owns the traditional land, and is managed and controlled by King Goodwill Zwelithini kaBhekuzulu on behalf of the state for the benefit of its occupants.

Amongst the improvements to the compound, the South African Department of Public Works built a helipad, underground bunkers, and accommodation for his private security, a so-called and highly controversial 'fire' (swimming) pool, a chicken-run, and fenced in the entire compound. It appeared that a surplus of R200,000,000 had been allocated by the department, and labeled it as 'questionable security renovations' especially since the department is limited to spending R100,000 on security improvements at private residences of public officials.

Alice VL

A spokesperson pointed out an apartheid-era law, the National Key Points Act, to justify the spending discrepancy. The leaked documentation hinted at enormously inflated prices for the so-called work done at Nkandla, and it noted that the work done never made it to tender stage and included massive consulting fees. (340) Public Protector Thuli Madonsela's final report on security upgrades to the compound, titled "Secure in comfort," was published in March 2014.

In both the provisional and final reports, Thuli Madonsela found that Jacob Zuma had benefited unduly from the R246M that the state had paid for Nkandla's upgrades. (341)

The South African Police Service prevented Helen Zille from the DA from 'seeing' what a R246M renovation of public funds looked like. Jacob Zuma's spokesperson, Mac Maharaj stated that it was clear that the opposition party adopted a 'cowboy style' approach, and questioned Helen Zille's use of the word 'compound' to describe Jacob Zuma's home. (342) However, in May 2015, South African Police Minister Nkosinathi Nhleko who was appointed by Jacob Zuma in May 2014 released his findings regarding the Nkandla compound. It stated that the 'fire' (swimming) pool, cattle kraal, chicken-run, visitor's center, and amphitheater were much-needed security features for Nkandla. The conclusion of the report stated that Jacob Zuma did not owe the South African public and taxpayers a refund.

Jacob Zuma was previously charged with various counts of racketeering, money laundering, corruption, and fraud. The included twelve counts of fraud, four counts of corruption, one count of money laundering and one count of racketeering but were dropped in 2009. (343) In December 2017, President Jacob Zuma had 18 charges of fraud and corruption against him. (344) (345)

The auditing firm, KPMG was hired by the National Prosecuting Authority to conduct a forensic accounting investigation before Schabir Shaik's trial. The extent of the auditing investigation was then extended to include additional factors, as well as a detailed analysis of Jacob Zuma's financial position. The investigation found that 'Jacob Zuma experienced financial difficulties from as early as January 1995.' It was clear that he was in no way in a position to settle his debts or meet his financial obligations and had to rely on other 'sources.' The auditing firm identified 783 payments made to, and on behalf of Jacob Zuma by Schabir Shaik and his Nkobi group between 1995 and 2006. The payments totaled in excess of R4-million. Jacob Zuma insists that he never committed any crime. After spending an estimated R15M on legal fees which was funded by South African taxpayers, it is unclear whether he will ever face prosecution. (346)

According to President Cyril Ramaphosa, the decision to fund Jacob Zuma's legal battle was made because the crimes he stands accused of were 'of public import.' President Ramaphosa justified his statement by saying that the presidency believed at the time of concluding the 2006 'fees deal' with Jacob Zuma, that the crimes he was accused of committing 'were in regard to his duties' as a parliamentary official. Again, the taxpayers become poorer as we pay for the defense of crimes against ALL South Africans. (347) (348)

Alice VL

MATAMELA CYRIL RAMAPHOSA
Current SA President

Born 17 November 1952, Cyril Ramaphosa is the current President of South Africa. He is the former Chairman of the National Planning Commission, responsible for the strategic planning for the future of the country. Cyril Ramaphosa developed the largest and most powerful trade union in South Africa known as the National Union of Mineworkers (NUM). He played a crucial role, along with Roelf Meyer of the National Party when they engaged in the negotiations to bring about a peaceful end to apartheid, steering South Africa towards its first fully democratic elections in April 1994.

He previously held prominent ownership in companies such as McDonald's South Africa and he was chair of the board for MTN and member of the board for Lonmin. Despite the fact that he was an invaluable component of South Africa's transition to democracy, he has been criticized for the way he conducts business even though he has never been charged for any illegal activities. Amongst his controversial business dealings, is his joint venture with Glencore together with allegations that he benefited illegally from coal deals with Eskom, which he has strongly denied.

When the Marikana Massacre took place at Lonmin's location, Cyril Ramaphosa was an active board of director and on 15 August 2012, he called for action against the miners engaging in the Marikana strike. He called it 'dastardly criminal' conduct that needed 'concomitant action' to be taken. He later admitted and regretted his involvement in the massacre and said that it could have been avoided if proper contingency plans had been made prior to the strike.

The Marikana massacre took place when the South African Police Service dispersed a group of striking Lonmin miners near Nkaneng in Marikana on 16 August 2012. As a result of police shootings, 34 miners died, and an additional 78 were injured, resulting in anger and frustration against the police and the South African government, especially when it emerged that most of the miners were shot in the back and from a distance by the police.

During the subsequent Marikana Commission, it emerged that Lonmin management had implored Cyril Ramaphosa to coordinate 'concomitant action' against 'criminal' protesters. He is therefore thought by many to be responsible for the massacre. (349) (350)

Among other positions, he is executive chairman of Shanduka Group, a company he founded that holds investments in various sectors such as the resources sector, energy sector, real estate, banking, insurance, and telecoms (SEACOM). (351)

In August 2017, Cryil Ramaphosa was involved in a scandal which accused him of being in several extramarital affairs. He was also accused of financially rewarding these women while engaging in these affairs. Cryil Ramaphosa later denied the claims saying they were politically motivated to derail his presidential campaign. (352) (353) (354)

Shortly after Cyril Ramaphosa became South Africa's deputy president, he lashed out at companies he accused of making profits disappear by moving them 'to low-tax operations where there is little or no genuine activity.' However, it was later revealed through a joint investigation by amaBhungane and Finance Uncovered (a global investigative journalism network) that MTN, Africa's largest mobile phone company, moved billions of rands that were earned in African countries to offshore tax havens while Cryil Ramaphosa chaired its board between 2001 and 2013. Most of the money which MTN marked as 'management fees,' ended up on the Island of Mauritius, where the company employs no staff and appears to own nothing more than a postal box. (355)

On the peace-promoting South African National Anthem, Cyril Ramaphosa had much to say. 'I don't believe that social cohesion in our country is falling apart. We come from a fractured past, and we've got wounds that need to continue being healed and some of the wounds revolve around the national anthem.' Cyril Ramaphosa described as unfortunate the controversies over "Die Stem" when Afrikaans singer Steve Hofmeyr sang the old national anthem in Australia, and the EFF called for the "Die Stem" portion of the current anthem and be removed from the official national anthem. (356)

Alice VL

MR. PRESIDENT, THE COWARD

Each time he opens his mouth, we get angrier. Our people get angrier. South Africa gets angrier. At first, I would swallow my retort, and just listen to the deceptions and defamations that spills from his mouth, shake my head, and slide into the next day. Each new day, he would deny our pain, our suffering, and the hunt that is on for us. Perhaps by his command? And every single day, it gets worse. He empowers himself like a coward does, through our silence. His spineless silence condemns the reality of our extinction, and it angers us, and it surges by the hour.

It's hard for others to imagine what it is like to live in our time. He is nothing more than a front for the mob, the cartels and the war lords who have steadily taken over South Africa, leaving destruction in their wake with nothing more than the ruins of their greed, their hatred, and their hunt for our blood. The friendly face he portrays to keep us and the rest of the world pacified is long gone. He no longer has a need to hide his abhorrence. There is no repercussion or punishment for his actions. It is out in the open, and the world knows. His failure to

Alice VL

protect us or condemn the crimes against us must be his fiercest message so far. Like the true coward he is, he insists that the torturous murders against us are merely 'internet crimes,' fabricated online, and spread throughout the world by the malicious minority; us.

We no longer use the word 'government' as a respected or authoritive organization. We have lost our taste for being dominated, crippled, hunted and murdered. Nevertheless, some of our own still can't see. They don't hear. They don't understand. They don't condemn. Instead, some of us bow to his commands, and bow to their hatred. He has the world believe that we are racists, or as he famously and regularly says, 'white supremacists' for speaking out against him, and his terrorist government; against the forces out to destroy us, and in direct opposition of our Christianity.

Yet, the very religions of his and his terrorist armies have inspired crude methods of control, allowing him the puppeteer, the grand master, the greatest coward, to hide behind false superiority while manipulating his kind into barbarous acts of war, genocide and culture murders. The world *knows* this. We know this. But remaining silent, makes his manipulation simpler. We won't remain silent any longer. We can't bow down to their acts of terrorism, and we don't fear him or his evil ways. We fear only

Alice VL

our God.

Mr. President, our government, suppressors, and anti-genocide promoters have learnt how to influence and control the subconscious minds of their followers, bypassing their own ability to make decisions, and indoctrinating their minds with false truths, false history and his own personal, cowardly narrative.

We can no longer surrender to their terrorist agendas. We don't. We won't. Ever. We choose to fight by using the methods of generations before us; not for counterpropaganda, but to free our minds from their nauseating enclosures of fear.

Morals aren't principles given how he bends them to suit himself, yet there is no need to for him to be authentic. Like a weakling. Like a coward. We intend and have begun to move in the right direction with certainty and pride, towards a day when our country's needs are effectively met, and with superior integrity and morals. Because the right to freedom, and lead a natural life is God given to all. It's up to us to make a society where that can happen. And we will.

Resource restriction is their choice of weapon for this war. A way to cause stress in a selected and targeted population with enough tension to bring about conflict. Restriction of any need such as employment, protection against his criminal entities, and the right to life will undoubtedly lead to war. A war they are calling for. A war his tribe is counting on. A war they cannot win because, even the most vigorous of cultures will become contaminated once they are refused their basic needs. And they will. Eventually.

By placing us in 'survival mode,' they have placed us on the path to retaliation with a strong desire to survive by any force necessary. And we will. We've been here before. We've walked down this road before. We've dealt with terrorism and evil before. We will again.

He is in power because he craves it, yet, he is the least suitable to lead us. He is nothing more than a power-hungry sociopath. And if by any chance the president deems this to be untrue, stand up, and tell the world what the true state of South Africa is. Tell them that you have lost control. Tell them that your loyalty was bought a long time ago; first by the very terrorist organization you helped form, and then by the corporations that fed your greed. You don't represent us. You don't represent our country. You will never represent our tribe. You are a coward.

Alice VL

SOUTH AFRICAN POLICE SERVICE CRIMES AND CORRUPTION

While crime is out of control in South Africa, case dockets disappear from police stations, police officers are involved in crimes, weapons are 'stolen' from police stations, and farmers are brutally murdered, we are assured of the fact that our police officers are committed to fighting crime and upholding the South African law.

But, *all* South Africans aren't protected or safeguarded. *All* South Africans are not in a position to rely on the South African Police to uphold the laws of the country and in the end, most South Africans fail to report crimes, and distrust in the police force increases as it becomes clear that the law is no longer designed to protect *all* South Africans *equally*.

The South African Police Service recently disclosed and conceded to the fact that hundreds of serving police officers are convicted criminals. The numbers are appalling and equally shocking, but they fail to reveal the full extent of criminal behavior in the police force.

Alice VL

In 2014, the South African Police Service revealed that a 'protracted' and 'thorough' audit of the police's grades had revealed that over a thousand serving police officers were convicted criminals.

They conceded to the fact that these members of the South African Police Service were all convicted of serious crimes and ranged from murder, attempted murder, rape, assault, corruption, theft, robbery, house-breaking, drug trafficking, domestic violence and aiding escapees. Of the 1,448 police officers that were convicted of crimes, at least 64 officers were based at Police Headquarters. (357)

In recent years, the South African Police Service has seen a number of devastating corruption scandals. Jackie Selebi was appointed as Police Commissioner in 2000 by Thabo Mbeki, South Africa's then-president. He maintained his position until 2008 when he was placed on an extended leave of absence following corruption allegations. (358) In addition to his role as Police Commissioner, Jackie Selebi was a former member of South Africa's Parliament, a former South African Ambassador to the United Nations, President of Interpol. In 2010, he was tried and convicted of taking bribes from a drug trafficker and sentenced to 15 years in prison. He was later released for medical reasons after serving a mere 229 days of his sentence. Not surprising considering that he ordered the South African Police Service's Anti-Corruption Unit (ACU) to be shut down, a mere seven years into operation. (359)

From the period 1996 up to 2001, in excess of twenty thousand allegations and complaints of corruption in the police force were received by the ACU. Between 1995 and 1999, roughly 1,300 South African Police Service members were convicted of crimes. Gareth Newham, Head of the Governance, Crime, and Justice Division at South Africa's Institute for Security Studies, has since revealed that there is evidence to suggest that 'most police officers involved in criminality are not being held accountable.' This means that the numbers of police officers involved in crimes are much higher than the initial number.

Between 1998 and 2012, at least 21,000 criminal cases which excludes deaths in custody or misconduct, but that involved police officers, were reported to South Africa's Independent Complaints Directorate (ICD), a civilian oversight structure and recently re-named as the Independent Police Investigative Directorate (IPID). According to the South African Independent Complaints Directorate's annual reports, in excess of 2,000 criminal cases involving the South African Police were reported each year since 2007.

Alice VL

For the year 2011/2012, the ICD's annual report revealed that 1,050 South African Police Service members were formally charged with corruption, fraud, aiding escapees, defeating the ends of justice, extortion and bribery. Only 88 of those members were suspended pending the outcome of their investigations. Another 1,286 cases of corruption were investigated. Police Minister Bheki Cele has revealed that there are at least another twenty-seven officers of South Africa's Crime Intelligence Division who have criminal records. 'Twenty members' criminal records relate to contraventions of the Road Traffic Act, whilst seven of a serious nature.' (360) (361) (362)

In Ficksburg – Free State, ten police officers, and five Home Affairs officials were among eighteen that were arrested for fraud and corruption at the border of Lesotho. After a year of intensive planning, The Hawks, the South African Police Service, South African Crime Intelligence and Home Affairs conducted a raid and found that the officers were supplying fraudulent permits and passports to Basotho nationals. (363)

In June 2018, a Tshwane Metro Police Officer was arrested following a police investigation into the spate of cash-in-transit heists. She is said to have been involved with the attack of two cash in transit vehicles. The officer was charged with aiding and abetting, and for storing weapons related to multiple cash-in-transit robberies. The officer's boyfriend was accused of being the ringleader of the operation and was believed to be involved with a number of prior cash in transit heists. According to the news network, News24, when they had raided her home, an automatic rifle along with ammunition was discovered. (364)

After a security clearance fiasco regarding a Police Brigadier, it was later discovered that he had joined the police force after being convicted of theft. Khehla Sitole, Portfolio Committee National Police Commissioner, said that Crime Intelligence Brigadier Leonora Phetlhe has since been suspended, but that she was challenging the suspension.

Bonang Mgwenya who is Deputy National Commissioner for Human Resource Management has since stated that the lack of technology was to blame when Brigadier Leonora Phethle was first employed. 'When this matter was raised, we then went into the records. Indeed, we did find she had a conviction in 1997. However, when she was enlisted, the system at the time could not pick it up. She was enlisted two years after conviction. At the time our systems were not yet advanced. We have a number of systems in place now.' (365)

Fugitive Crime Intelligence Officer Morris 'KGB' Tshabalala was dismissed by the South African Police Service when he was denied bail by the Pretoria Specialised Commercial Crime Court for plundering the Crime Intelligence Unit of in excess of R 500,000. At his court appearance, it was revealed that he did not surrender to the Department of Correctional Services in 1996 to begin serving a 10-year jail sentence for an armed robbery he committed in 1994 in Mamelodi, Pretoria. During that time, he was convicted of the illegal possession of an unlicensed firearm and ammunition in addition to the robbery charges.

In 2013, he was arrested in a raid connecting him to a R3-million cash-in-transit heist, but he was later acquitted of the crime. State Prosecutor Chris Smith told the court that when police processed Morris Tshabalala's fingerprints after his 2013 arrest, they only then discovered that he was being sought since 1998. In 2015, Morris Tshabalala was released on parole, and despite the fact that he was dismissed from the South African Police Service, he remained on the South African Police Service payroll and continued to receive a monthly salary. While out on parole, he re-enlisted in the covert Crime Intelligence Unit of the South African Police Service and maintains the rank of Police Captain. (366)

In Johannesburg, one of three police officers were found guilty of murder after the death of robbery suspect, Khulekani Mpanza. The court found that Titus Mabela shot Khulekani

Mpanza unlawfully while he was unarmed and lying on the ground. A video of his murder went viral and resulted in angry outbursts which prompted calls for an investigation into police brutality. The second accused, Puleng Sebetwa, was found guilty of assault for kicking Khulekani Mpanza, who did not fight back. Jason Segole, the third accused, was acquitted on all charges. (367)

The Independent Police Investigative Directorate's (IPID) half-yearly report in 2016 revealed that thousands of cases of police brutality are reported in South Africa each year, but only a fraction of them ever result in criminal charges. 'IPID tracks deaths while in police custody, or as a result of police action, police shootings rapes committed by officers, complaints of torture or assault against police officers, and accusations of corruption within the police force.' (368)

In the case of a taxi driver, Mido Macia who died after being handcuffed to and dragged behind a police vehicle, eight policemen were found guilty of his murder. He was initially arrested for parking his car on the wrong side of the road which resulted in a traffic jam. Witnesses at the trial stated that the taxi driver was beaten after being dragged through the streets. A pathologist testified that the possible three-hour delay in seeking medical assistance for him resulted in the fact that he died. (369) (370)

Alice VL

Traffic Officer, Reginald Heinrich Carolus appeared in the Bellville Specialized Commercial Crimes Court for accusations of fraud, corruption and defeating the ends of justice. He was accused of assisting a learner license applicant in obtaining a learner's license without subjecting the person to the test. 'Additionally, he unduly assisted a motorist in acquiring a roadworthy certificate for a vehicle that never went through a mandatory test, despite him not being a designated official in dealing with testing of vehicles.' The court stated. (371)

A 57-year-old traffic officer employed by the Gauteng Traffic Department appeared in the Pretoria Commercial Crimes Court on charges of corruption and extortion. In a joint sting operation by the Road Traffic Management Corporation's National Traffic Anti-Corruption Unit, the Tshwane Metro Police Internal Affairs Unit and the Gauteng Traffic Department's Compliance Unit, a principal provincial inspector was arrested. 'The arrest followed a complaint received through the RTMC's hotline with allegations that the officer was removing motor vehicle license discs and taking driving licenses from motorists on the pretext that they had committed a traffic offense. The victims would then allegedly be instructed to deliver a sum of money ranging from R1,500 to the officer at the regional offices of the provincial traffic department in exchange for their documents.'

Alice VL

the Road Traffic Management Corporation said. (372)

Another Traffic Officer was charged with attempted murder when he opened fire on three teenage girls, and injuring one of them in Greenside, Polokwane. Police spokesperson Colonel Moatshe Ngoepe said the girls, aged 13, 15 and 17, were walking alongside a road when the officer began insulting them from his vehicle. 'An exchange of words ensued between the man and the youngsters until he chased them with his motor vehicle. The suspect apparently fired several shots in the direction of the children, injuring the 17-year-old in the process. Police and emergency services were alerted, leading to the apprehension of the suspect and the confiscation of his private firearm.' Colonel Ngoepe said. (373)

A Metro Police Department Traffic Officer was arrested for taking a R300 bribe from a truck driver, the Road Traffic Management Corporation (RTMC) said. 'Investigations were initiated following a video that went viral on social media earlier this week showing what appears to be an owner of a trucking company accusing traffic officers of extorting a bribe from his truck driver on Vereeniging Road in Alberton, in Ekurhuleni spokesman Simon Zwane said. (374)

An additional eleven traffic officers were arrested for

corruption in Limpopo, the Road Traffic Management Corporation said. Spokesperson Simon Zwane said the Road Traffic Management Corporation's National Traffic Anti-Corruption Unit and the Hawk's Serious Corruption Crime Unit arrested the officers in their campaign to phase out bribery and corruption in the traffic law enforcement unit. 'The officers, aged between 32 and 54, were arrested following intensive investigations into the allegation of bribery and unethical conduct among traffic officers in the province. The latest arrests bring the total number of traffic officers arrested in this province to 33 since December 2017.' (375)

Photographs are regularly circulated across media and news sites that show members of the South African Police Service asleep at their precincts or in their patrol cars; police stations that were, are and will continue to be robbed of their weapons, while others are boldly attacked. (376)

An R5 rifle and two empty magazines were stolen in a robbery at the Eden Park police station in the early hours on a Thursday morning. Gauteng police spokesperson Brigadier Mathapelo Peters said that the two men walked into the police station shortly after midnight and ordered police officers on duty in the Client Service Centre to hand over the keys to the safe. (377)

Alice VL

In February 2018, five policemen were killed during an attack on a police station in Ngcobo. South African Police Service reported that a Warrant Officer and four constables were shot and killed. Three South African Police Service members were shot on location while two additional members were kidnapped before being killed and left on the side of the road. An off-duty soldier was shot and killed as the attackers fled the scene. Two additional male officers were wounded and transferred to hospital. (378)

In June 2017, Hillbrow Police Station was robbed while 11 on-duty police officers were asleep. South African Police Service has since dismissed and strongly denied reports that the officers were sleeping. (379)

Other pictures show images of police officers out shopping in patrol cars or vans with friends, family and/or acquaintances. (380)

Photos of an inebriated police officer in Pietermaritzburg behind the wheel of a police service vehicle with a bottle of alcohol between his legs were circulated on social media in 2015. In January 2013, another intoxicated police officer was arrested by a civil citizen who locked him in the back of his own service vehicle after witnessing him drive recklessly through the streets of Pietermaritzburg in Kwazulu Natal. (381)

In March 2015, a video of yet another policeman who was inebriated behind the wheel while his service weapon was on his lap, went viral on social media. The man who filmed the video questioned the officer at the side of the road in Durban, before the officer sped off. (382)

THE PRESIDENT'S 'HAND-PICKED' HOUSE OF OFFENDERS

Only recently did my president, Cyril Ramaphosa announce to the world that he is committed to sifting out all forms of corruption and crime in government, and that he aims to deal harshly with public officials who engage in any form of corruption. Yet, we are faced with the fact that the majority of his cabinet has been involved in disgraces and felonies, a house he hand-picked and selected while fully aware of their past criminal and scandalous activities.

Deputy President—David Mabuza

David Mabuza has been accused of corruption, involvement in tender fraud and for being behind the assassination of political opponents while acting as premier of Mpumalanga. In 2015, he was supposedly poisoned but recovered. He was since given the nickname 'The Cat' for his ability to survive attacks by his opponents. In 2010, a large sum of cash estimated at the time to be to the value of R14 million was stolen from his home. The provincial organized crime unit insisted only R1,200 was stolen from his home, but he later reported only R4-million missing. He felt that reporting the entire R14 million would raise eyebrows and therefore, only reported R4 million as stolen. (383)

David Mabuza has said that allegations against him were nothing more than part of a smear campaign. He says the fact that the Guptas once airlifted him to receive medical assistance in Russia does not mean that he owes them anything. 'He wants them held accountable' he responded when questioned on what government plans to do concerning board members of state-owned companies who were implicated in allegations of state capture.

EFF's Hlengiwe Hlope-Maxon specifically questioned him on how he was assisting law enforcement in tracing the controversial Gupta family 'who arranged a Gupta jet for you to go to Russia?' when he received specialized medical care following allegations that he was poisoned. (384) The man who took out a protection order against David Mabuza enlisted forensic investigator Paul O'Sullivan's services to pursue criminal charges against him. Jan Venter was the topic of discussion in South Africa when he became a central figure in a R10-million defamation lawsuit that David Mabuza instituted against former

ANC treasurer-general Mathews Phosa. Jan Venter worked as Matthews Phosa's butler, but after a bitter labor dispute, he told David Mabuza that he witnessed Matthews Phosa and his associate, Nick Elliot, concocting an intelligence report that claimed David Mabuza was an apartheid spy.

The report stated that David Mabuza spied on ANC leaders, including former president Jacob Zuma, and reported their activities to the apartheid government. Jan Venter successfully obtained an interim protection order against David Mabuza after claiming that he received threats from an unknown number at the time he planned a media conference to expose the fact that David Mabuza paid him to testify for him. Payments to him included cash amounts, a car, and a firearm. (385)

Then, there are the allegations that David Mabuza was behind a number of political killings in Mpumalanga. It is speculated that David Mabuza was behind the arrest of a journalist who published articles about an unknown man who claimed he was employed by provincial officials to act as an assassin. (386)

The question all South Africans ask is; how is President Cyril Ramaphosa operating alongside such a character? Besides the R14 million that was stolen from his home, the allegations against Deputy President, David Mabuza is astonishing. Mathews Phosa said in an interview with the eNCA that David Mabuza was employing a private army to intimidate ANC members opposed to his so-called unity campaign. A video showed a group of men wearing caps dancing outside a house. It is said that three men pulled out firearms and fired off multiples of shots into the air in a crowd that included children. (387)

David Mabuza has been accused of being behind several political killings, specifically in his province. Among the murdered is Mbombela speaker Jimmy Mohlala, who was killed in 2009. Jimmy Mohlala blew the whistle on tender corruption regarding a stadium built for the 2010 Fifa Soccer World Cup. It is surmised that James Nkambule, another whistleblower, was also poisoned for claiming politicians were behind the assassinations. (388) (389)

David Mabuza was accused of being behind the awarding of many tenders to friends and family. Sizwangendaba Investment, a company owned by a friend and former business partner of David Mabuza, was awarded a multimillion-rand tender to provide agricultural appliances to farmers in the province. (390)

Minister of Finance—Nhlanhla Nene

Nhlanhla Nene was active in student politics in the 1970s and became a member of the African National Congress (ANC) Regional Executive Committee, Bambatha region, where he was Chairperson of the Bambatha Branch, the head of South Africa's state asset manager, the Public Investment Corporation (PIC).

Dan Matjila was accused of using his influence to thrust financial support in the direction of a love interest. According to Matjila, the smear campaign was the work of corrupt individuals who had been trying to get their hands on state support and failed. (391)

Nhlanhla Nene, the Finance Minister who was dismissed by Jacob Zuma because he was in the way of looting state assets, had promised Matjila his full backing. Nhlanhla Nene, who was reinstated by President Cyril Ramaphosa, has refused to suspend Matjila as a political party had requested. (392)

Deputy Minister of Finance—Mondli Gungubele

'The ANC needs to act against its 'ill-disciplined' MP Mondli Gungubele for saying he will not vote against the motion of no confidence against President Jacob Zuma.' Chief Whip, Jackson Mthembu. 'Comrade Mondli Gungubele has become the latest ANC MP to join a defiance campaign to publicly pronounce that he will not vote according to the ANC party line in the upcoming motion of no confidence in President Zuma by the opposition in Parliament.' he said in a statement. (393)

Under his leadership, a number of scandals were exposed and does not include a number of smaller corruption and mismanagement allegations or his extravagant expenditure.

- The illegal appointment of city manager, Khaya Ngema.

- Awarding an IT tender worth R35-million.

- Awarding a tender for the procurement of water meters worth R205–million.

- Awarding a tender for an 'institutional review' for R32-million.

- Awarding R100-million worth of tenders in the Roads and Transport Department.

- Snubbing the Constitutional Court ruling on the illegal removal and relocation of over 1000 people from Babsfontein to the N12 informal settlement.

- A number of police chiefs who were either not qualified or under criminal investigation. (394)

Alice VL

Minister of Energy—Jeff Radebe

Jeff Radebe begged a 29-year-old member of staff to send him pictures of her private parts. The Sunday Times published an article of how presidential photographer, Siyasanga Mbambai was sent text messages from 64-year-old Jeff Radebe dating back to 2014. The newspaper published samples of the texts, which included Jeff Radebe imploring her to do more than just send him a picture of herself fully clothed. She later sent him a photograph of herself in a bubble bath, where she showed her naked breasts. 'Let me see there,' a later text from him was sent telling her that he was interested in a picture of herself 'further down.' She says she refused to send him such a photograph. In one X-rated message he sent her, Jeff Radebe demanded, 'C.l.i.t is requested.'

Initially, Siyasanga denied that she sent him pictures of herself, but later admitted to it when she was confronted with proof. 'I might have been drunk and got tired of him asking for my pictures, so I just sent them.' She was quoted as saying. (395)

Minister of State Security—Dipuo Letsatsi-Duba

A secret state spy fund was reportedly used to spend

R10-million on a luxury mansion that was to become the new home of the State Security Minister after she discarded the house made available by the government. According to The Sunday Times, Minister Dipuo Letsatsi-Duba personally negotiated the purchase of the Waterkloof home following a meeting with an estate agent and the owner of the house.

Minister Letsatsi-Duba rejected the government-approved home she was offered and complained about 'maintenance challenges.' She personally approved the deviation from the Supply Chain Management process by signing off on R10-million from the State Security Agency's slush fund to cover the cost of the house and furniture.

The agency denied that the house was specifically bought for the Minister but admitted it was among a number of options being considered. Over the years, the agency has been accused of spending an exorbitant amount of funds to buy luxury vehicles and residential properties for its officials. In addition, they have been accused of 'forking out a fortune' as payments to so-called 'ghost informers' who turned out to be related to top management. (396) (397)

Minister of Public Enterprises—Pravin Gordhan

Alice VL

In October 2016, South Africa's state prosecutor brought fraud charges against Pravin Gordhan for allowing a former colleague at the South African Revenue Service to enjoy early retirement and then re-employing the same colleague as a consultant. However, the charges were dropped a few days later.

In September 2017, KPMG auditing firm abruptly withdrew all its findings, recommendations and conclusions around a report into the South African Revenue Service (SARS) 'rogue spy unit' which directly implicated Pravin Gordhan. SARS Commissioner Tom Moyane disputed KPMG's withdrawal, calling it 'unethical conduct,' and claimed that the report was not flawed. (398) (399)

Minister of Home Affairs—Malusi Gigaba

When an offshore bank account was opened in then Public Enterprises Minister Malusi Gigaba's name in the United Arab Emirates, he claimed that the account was opened by one of his officials without his knowledge or approval. Following an investigation, banking and security officials insist that it's impossible for anyone to open an offshore account using another person's identity without their knowledge.

In a court judgment relating to the Fireblade Aviation

case in October 2017, the North Gauteng High Court found that Malusi Gigaba lied under oath. The judge lashed out at him, and called his arguments 'disingenuous, spurious and fundamentally flawed, labored and meritless, bad in law, astonishing, palpably untrue, untenable and not sustained by objective evidence, uncreditworthy and nonsensical.'

The appointment of Malusi Gigaba as Minister of Public Enterprises, initiating the 'repurposing' of State-Owned Enterprises as instruments for pillaging was the primary point in the state capture report. It included the appointment of Iqbal Sharma, a Gupta acquaintance, to the Transnet board as did it Brian Molefe, another known associate of the Guptas, as Transnet chief executive in 2011.

In July 2012, Anoj Singh was appointed as Chief Financial Officer for Transnet, placing all procurement under him. Almost immediately, Transnet issued a tender for 1,064 freight locomotives: 599 electric and the remainder diesel. This included R25-billion in tenders that were awarded to China South Rail.

China South Rail, in turn, paid Tequesta Group Ltd which is a Gupta-linked shell company R5.3-billion in so-called 'consultancy fees.' Malusi Gigaba was appointed as the Public Enterprises Minister in 2009, 'Eskom had R19-billion in cash.

Alice VL

When he left in 2014, Eskom was penniless.'

Soon after his appointment, he settled on new appointments and agreed to employ them whether or not they had previous corporate or electricity sector experience. With Eskom now captured and restructured, the Guptas were free to engage in brokering and money laundering. The Gupta's Tegeta Exploration and Resources benefited from an Eskom guarantee for R1.6-billion, plus a pre-payment of R600-million and further profitable coal contracts which enabled the purchase of Optimum. (400) (401) (402)

Minister of International Relations—Lindiwe Sisulu

In 1990, Lindiwe Sisulu was assistant to Jacob Zuma in the ANC's intelligence services. Her housing project labeled as the N2 Gateway was the basis of a number of uncomfortable debates. The Joe Slovo Informal Settlement adamantly refused to be relocated to Delft in Cape Town, in order to make way for government housing. After a protest by Joe Slovo residents, Lindiwe Sisulu blatantly stated that 'if they choose not to cooperate with the government, they will be completely removed from all housing waiting lists.'

In December 2007, the N2 Gateway hosted the largest

occupation of houses in the country's history which resulted in the displacement of thousands of families into temporary relocation areas and onto the pavement in Symphony Way. In September 2009, she appointed Paul Ngobeni as her legal advisor who was at once challenged by Parliament's Standing Committee on Public Accounts (SCOPA) and the Standing Committee on Defence. Paul Ngobeni was not qualified to practice law in South Africa and had been disbarred from practicing law in the United States where he faced criminal charges of fraud, larceny, and petty theft. (403)

In addition, Lindiwe Sisulu was accused of abusing executive jet flights during her tenure as Minister of Defence and Military Veterans where she made 203 trips with the South African Air Force rented Gulfstream plane. However, when an apology was issued citing incorrect figures, it was discovered that she had made only 35 trips. (404)

In April 2013, she appointed Menzi Simelane as her legal advisor, who in October 2012, was found unfit to be appointed as head of the National Prosecuting Authority by South African Constitutional Court Judge, Zac Jacoob. '[We] conclude that the evidence was contradictory and on its face indicative of Mr. Simelane's honesty. It raises serious questions about Mr. Simelane's conscientiousness, integrity, and credibility.' (405)

Alice VL

Deputy Minister of International Relations—Regina Mhaule

A 62-year-old domestic worker who was employed by Regina Mhaule filed a case of fraud against her after she discovered that someone might have been pocketing her government-issued salary without her knowledge. Linah Mkhabela, who worked as a cleaner for Reginah since 2009, said she was unaware that she had been a government employee since she received her R2 000 monthly salary in cash. 'I thought that the MEC was doing me a favor because we were going to the same church, but when I applied for an old age pension at the South African Social Security Agency, I was told that I do not qualify because I had been a government employee.'

Official government documents seen by an unnamed journalist show that Linah Mkhabela was in fact on the payroll of the Department of Public Works, Roads and Transport, and is responsible for the maintenance of government houses on behalf of Mpumalanga politicians who use state housing. The documents show that Linah was earning a salary of between R71 289 and R87 330 per year between August 1, 2012, and June 30, 2014. She claims she never received a salary reflecting those amounts, or a payslip to show that she was a government employee during that period. She says the only salary she ever received was R2 000, which was given to her in cash by an official in Regina Mhaule's office. (406)

Minister of Public Works—Thulas Nxesi

Minister of public works Thulas Nxesi, then part of a 13-member 'Non-Aligned Movement Committee on Palestine,' was prevented from entering Palestine in 2012.

They were scheduled to meet in Ramallah in August 2012 but were barred from entering Palestine by Israel due to a lack of diplomatic relations with Israel. Minister Nxesi, who is a vocal pro-Palestinian supporter has endorsed Israeli Apartheid Week over the years, saying, 'If we keep quiet, it would mean we support what these killers are doing.' (407)

Minister of Water and Sanitation—Gugile Nkwinti

South African land reforms remain a challenging issue especially since Gugile Nkwinti stated that funds are unavailable to reach their target of redistributing 30% of land back to black South Africans by 2014. Instead, he advocated for a policy of reforming the approximate 90% of reclaimed, unproductive land.

Alice VL

He has bluntly said that commercial South African farmers must co-operate or share a fate 'worse than Zimbabwe' and has previously suggested the policy of land expropriation without compensation. (408)

Minister of Transport—Blade Nzimande

Blade Nzimande was vocal in criticizing Thabo Mbeki's rule, along with his economic policy and supported his removal as president of South Africa. When interim-president Kgalema Motlanthe dismissed refused to sign the SABC bill in 2008 giving the ANC full control of national television, he was under severe attack by Blade Nzimande.

In October 2017, Blade Nzimande was removed from his position as Minister of Higher Education and Training and replaced by Hlengiwe Mkhize. However, President Ramaphosa reinstated Blade Nzimande as Minister of Transport in his cabinet reshuffle. (409)

Minister of Sports—Tokozile Xasa

Tokozile Xasa SA Tourism, a body under the Department of Tourism, spent R9.6 million on public relations services received from Bell Pottinger. During that time, the Gupta Family had employed Bell Pottinger to publicize racial division and anti-white sentiment in South Africa. (410)

Minister of Communications—Nomvula Mokonyane

As Water Affairs and Sanitation Minister, Nomvula Mokonyane leads South Africa's Lesotho Highlands Water Project. Initial timelines stated that the project would be completed in 2024 at a cost of R22-billion. However, due to delays directly ordered by Nomvula Mokonyane, the date of completion has been moved to 2025, and the budget has escalated to R26 billion who is funded solely by the South African taxpayer.

When accused of mal-administration in this project, Nomvula Mokonyane said that she delayed the project for reasons of transformation and that more black-owned companies should be involved.

A report by City Press found that a single company, LTE Consulting, was awarded contracts worth R5-billion in one year. LTE donated an estimated R3.5-million to the ANC in the months of May and June 2016 and stands to make an estimated R2.6-billion from this project. (411) (412)

Alice VL

Deputy Minister of Communications—Pinkie Kekana

Public Protector Thuli Madonsela said that the former Limpopo roads and transport MEC Pinky Kekana disobeyed the constitution and abused her position to 'settle political scores' for the benefit of Julius Malema. Her provisional report into the abuse of state power indicated that Pinkie Kekana had ordered an off-duty traffic officer to arrest Thandi Moraka, Julius Malema's rival at a Limpopo elective conference. Titled 'State Power-Political Games,' the report stated that Pinkie Kekana's conduct was 'improper' and amounted to 'mal-administration.'

'Kekana's conduct amounted to mal-administration, because she did not just report a crime, but abused her official position as MEC while attending a private party political event to set state resources in her department in motion to settle a political score,' (413)

Minister of Social Development—Susan Shabangu

Susan Shabangu, Minister of Social Development, has been a member of parliament who represents the ANC as far back as May 1994. In March 2003, she was charged with public indecency after a dispute with an airport security official in which she lifted her dress after repeatedly setting off a metal detector.

Alice VL

(414) (415)

In April 2008, in her role as Deputy Minister of Safety and Security, she told police officers to 'kill the bastards', referring to criminals. (416)

In August 2012, a total of 44 people, 34 of which were miners, were killed at Lonmin Platinum Mine near Rustenburg after police opened fire on striking staff belonging to the Association of Mineworkers and Construction Union (AMCU). After engaging all mining stakeholders in talks regarding the massacre, the Minister was asked why AMCU was not involved in the discussions. She then stated that she was not aware that AMCU was operating in the mining industry. (417) (418)

Minister of Mineral Resources—Gwede Mantashe

In February 2010, after Julius Malema was booed at a South African Communist Party's special conference in Polokwane, he called on Gwede Mantashe to resign. The National Union of Metalworkers of SA (NUMSA) publicly supported Gwede Mantashe who delivered the inaugural Violet Seboni Memorial lecture at the Johannesburg City Hall in April 2010, addressing corruption in the ANC. 'The new order [after 1994] inherited a well-entrenched value system that placed individual acquisition of wealth at the very center of the value system of our society as a whole.' (419) (420)

Minister of Cooperative Governance—Zweli Mkhize

In September 2017, Zweli Mkhize announced that he will accept the nomination to become the next president of the ANC at their December conference. 'This calls upon me to now set the record straight and be clear that it was Zweli Mkhize who was accused of recommending the food to President Zuma.'

Gayton McKenzie, the author of 'Kill Zuma by Any Means Necessary,' reacted to a letter written by a faction of the MKMVA (Umkhonto weSizwe Military Veterans Association) that claimed that ANC President Cyril Ramaphosa tried to poison then-president Jacob Zuma. 'My sources have confirmed that there was a plot to kill President Jacob Zuma. The plot involved feeding Zuma a piece of liver, or according to another version, a plate of vegetables.' Gayton McKenzie disclosed that the culprit was Dr. Zweli Mkhize. 'The liver or the vegetables had been poisoned and brought to the table from outside of Luthuli House to be served to the President.' (421)

She did clarify later that she never pointed a finger directly at Cyril Ramaphosa and reiterated that she had never said that he suggested the president try the food.

Minister of Science and Technology—Mmamoloko Kubayi-Ngubane

In 2017, Minister of Energy Mmamoloko Kubayi-Ngubane was accused of backtracking on an investigation into the sale of the country's oil reserves. She announced in Parliament that she would investigate the contentious sale by the Strategic Fuel Fund (SFF) in which 10-million barrels of the country's fuel reserve was sold for a fraction of the market price. Yet, she announced at a meeting that the investigation into the irregularities and corruption that took place during the sale of the reserves would be put on ice. (422) (423)

She profusely denied interfering in the recruiting of key executives at the SABC. However, she insists that the board of the SABC consult her for quality control purposes. (424) (425)

Minister of Police—Bheki Cele

General Bheki Cele was dismissed as National Police Chief in June 2012. 'I have decided to release General Cele from his duties.' Jacob Zuma told reporters in Pretoria.

Alice VL

He referred to the board of inquiry that was mandated to establish whether Bheki Cele acted immorally, dishonestly, or with an undeclared conflict of interest regarding two police lease deals signed with business tycoon Roux Shabangu. One was for a building in Pretoria, and the other for a building in Durban. 'The board has found General Cele to be unfit for office and has recommended his removal from office in terms of the provisions of section 8(6)(b)(v) of the South African Police Service Act No. 68 of 1995.' - Jacob Zuma.

Bheki Cele, who was under investigation for an amount of R1.7-billion that was spent on building leases that were unlawful and unfitting, was suspended but continued to receive his R1.3-million a year salary.

In April 2009, he was criticized for comments he made at a rally in KwaZulu-Natal regarding the Inkatha Freedom Party and its leader Mangosuthu Buthelezi. He hinted that the IFP propagation of unlawful weaponry was made in an environment of political violence in Kwazulu-Natal.

In September 2010, Bheki commented that officers of the South African Police Service were to 'shape up or ship out,' and 'when you walk down the street, people must envy your body.' (426)

Alice VL

Minister of Higher Education—Naledi Pandor

Naledi Pandor oversaw a complete revamp of the South African education system where she proposed reforms to the apparent failure of the implementation of Outcomes Based Education (OBE).

South Africa's Department of Basic Education has lowered the pass rate for mathematics to just 20% in an effort to keep children moving through the country's inept school system. Given the high number of children at risk of being held back because of their math-test scores, a departmental circular, published by the news website GroundUp, announced that students in grades seven, eight and nine who met all the minimum requirements to pass, not including mathematics, should be promoted to the next grade if they attained a minimum of 20% in mathematics. In the past, if learners obtained a score of below 40%, they would fail the grade. Teachers and education activists were appalled by the department's decision. They said that the department's decision sent out a message to thousands of students that they are simply incapable of mastering maths when they should rather be taking responsibility for poor resources and teaching methods. 'We are setting these children up for failure. Now we are sending children to the next grade, who didn't fully grasp the grade they were coming from.' A primary school teacher told GroundUp.

An insider revealed that the 'maximum four years in phase' policy was implemented where a pupil may not repeat more than one year in each three-year phase of compulsory schooling. If a pupil has already repeated a year, they are 'progressed' to the next grade whether or not they meet the promotion or pass criteria. (427)

Minister of Human Settlements—Nomaindia Mfeketo

She was the fourth woman, but the first black woman to become executive mayor of Cape Town and served from 1998 to 2000. In 2009, the Democratic Alliance claimed that Nomaindia received a custom built 'mansion' worth R8 million as part of a notorious government housing plan for ministers in Cape Town and Pretoria, even though she owned a private residence less than 10 km away. (428)

Minister of Small Business Development—Lindiwe Zulu

The Public Protector's office was asked to investigate Small Business Development Minister Lindiwe Zulu following her department's purchase of two luxury vehicles only a week before

Christmas. Two new BMW's valued in excess of R1.8-million were bought on December 20, 2017 for the Minister and her Deputy. The cars were marketed for businesspeople with the promise of state-of-the-art features including 'automated driving in situations such as traffic jams and slow-moving traffic or on long journeys.' (429)

Deputy Minister of Small Business Development— Cassel Mathale

Cassel Mathale was thought to have been part of a faction that he formed with former ANC Youth League leader Julius Malema to replace Jacob Zuma with then ANC deputy president Kgalema Motlanthe at the party's elective conference in Mangaung.

In June, the ANC's task team said that reports deciding to dismiss Cassel Mothale were untrue. 'Those reports are absolutely untrue. The task team has no authority to fire the premier. That decision lies with the President.' (430)

Minister of Public Service and Administration—Ayanda Dlodlo

In an interview, Ayanda Dlodlo said directors-general

Alice VL

were expected to act as ministerial advisers. 'No minister should have more than two [advisers] because you should rely on what the department has, and even at a lower level in the department there are subject matter experts, so why do you need a bloated office with a large number of advisers when the department has all the expertise and experts that you need ... to discharge your mandate?'

'We've gone above the ceiling ... it should be scary for South Africans, but maybe not to the unions. But to the general [population] that should be scary.'

'If you look at wages and think we take from grants to pay salaries, I don't know what we will do on the day that our people revolt against the government, its employees, and political parties. It has happened in many other countries.

The DA called on President Cyril Ramaphosa to reduce the size of his cabinet. The ministers and their deputies will earn R163.5-million in 2018 while the Department of Public Works has spent R188-million on purchasing thirty-three properties for ministers and their deputies. (431) (432)

Deputy Minister of Public Service and Administration— Dr. Chana Pilane-Majake

Alice VL

Public Protector Thuli Madonsela reported on claims that the Commission for Gender Equality withheld payments of its former Chief Executive's contribution to the provident fund were unsubstantiated.

The commission had excluded Dr. Chana Pilane-Majake when it paid middle management service (MMS) and senior management service (SMS) arrears of the employer's contribution to the provident fund. (433)

Minister Rural Development and Land Reform—Maite Nkoana-Mashabane

Maite Nkoana-Mashabane was appointed as Minister of International Relations and Cooperation by President Jacob Zuma in May 2009. Jacob Zuma disputed suggestions that employing Maite Nkoana-Mashabane was an odd appointment given the fact that he lacks 'foreign policy' experience. He responded by saying that 'the ANC knows the strengths of this comrade.' (434)

Minister of Tourism—Darek Hanekom

Derek Hanekom served three years in prison with his wife, Dr. Trish Hanekom for working with the ANC during the apartheid era. When they joined the ANC in 1980, Patricia and Derek Hanekom fed information such as the apartheid Defence Force's attempts to overthrow the Mozambican government. Both were arrested in 1983 where they were initially charged with high treason. However, the charge was reduced due to the international sensitivity of the case. (435)

Minister in the Presidency for Planning, Monitoring, and Evaluation—Nkosazana Dlamini Zuma

In July 2012, Nkosazana Dlamini-Zuma was elected as the first woman to lead the Organization of African Unity. She is President Jacob Zuma's ex-wife and was favored by him to succeed him both as President of the ANC and as President of South Africa.

Nkosazana Dlamini-Zuma was immensely disliked among African Unity officials for her seeming disregard, detachment, and absenteeism while her leadership as Chairperson was considered an unacceptable failure.

In April 2017, she was scorned for labeling protest marches against Jacob Zuma as 'rubbish' and for referring to them as examples of white privilege. Her verified Twitter account posted, 'This is what they are protecting ... hence some of us are not part of this rubbish. They must join us for the march for our land they stole...' She deleted the tweet shortly afterward and referred to the tweet as a 'fake-tweet.' (436)

In addition, there have been numerous claims that her election campaign was being funded by tobacco smugglers. (437) (438)

Minister for Women and Disability in the Presidency— Bathabile Dlamini

Bathabile Dlamini and thirteen ANC officials were implicated by the Directorate of Special Operations for the abuse of parliamentary travel vouchers. The South African media subsequently dubbed this the 'Travelgate' scandal. Her charge sheet stated that she knew the travel vouchers were only to be used for air travel. However, she used them to cover the costs of hotel accommodation and car rentals. She was eventually convicted of fraud after pleading guilty to more than R200,000 worth of misleading travel claims.

As a result, she lost her position as a Member of Parliament, but in December 2007, at the 52nd National Conference of the ANC, she was elected to the ANC's National Executive and National Working Committees. (439)

Alice VL

As Minister of Social Development, Bathabile Dlamini failed to implement the government's proposal to take over payments of South Africa's social grants by March 2017. The arrangement with Cash Paymaster Services at the time to distribute payments was about to run out and would have resulted in welfare recipients not receiving grant payments in April 2017.

She was criticized for her failure to act and her inability to contract a new service or to implement the insourcing of the service, however, in March 2017, the contract with Cash Paymaster Services was renewed for an additional two years. (440)

Chief Justice Mogoeng of the Constitutional Court held Bathabile Dlamini responsible for the crisis and said that there was no explanation for the incompetence displayed by her and SASSA. (441)

Yet, despite her failures, President Zuma's support of her did not dwindle, and in turn, Bothabile Dlamini supported Nkosazana Dlamini-Zuma in her campaign to succeed him as leader of the ANC and President of South Africa. She was criticized for not appearing before Parliament or before committee meetings during the grants crisis; she did not appear before the Standing Committee on Public Accounts (SCOPA) in which she had to account for the irregular expenditure of about R1-billion by SASSA during the 2016/2017 financial year. (442)

In May 2017, Bathabile Dlamini appeared before a SCOPA meeting where she was questioned about approximately R1-million that was spent on private 'VIP' security for her children which was paid for by SASSA. She said that 'some people understand government more than others,' and that she was compelled to resort to private security since 'government processes take a long period.' She claimed that despite the 'VIP' protection she received through the South African Police Service, her home was burgled on three separate occasions. (443)

Minister of Agriculture, Forestry and Fisheries—Senzeni Zokwana

On the 16th of August 2012, 34 miners were gunned down by the South African Police Service after they embarked on a lengthy strike demanding a wage increase 34 were shot and killed by the police, and ten were killed with protest actions leading up to the massacre – six mine workers, two policemen, and two Lonmin security officers. At the center of the Marikana tragedy in which 34 miners were shot and killed; excluding six more miners, two police officers and two Lonmin security officers that were killed in protest actions leading up the massacre was then NUM president Senzeni Zokwana. (444) (445) (446)

In March 2018, the Hawks were probing former president Jacob Zuma for accepting a R1-million cash bribe from a Western Cape abalone dealer, Deon Larry, in exchange for keeping Senzeni Zokwana in his cabinet. He has denied involvement in any unlawful conduct in the awarding of contracts for the processing and sale of confiscated abalone and scoffed at plans to raise money for the ANC through the Department of Agriculture, Forestry, and Fisheries. (447) (448)

Deputy Minister of Agriculture—Sfiso Buthelezi

Financial mismanagement charges were made against Sfiso Buthelezi, Deputy Finance Minister and Lucky Montana, former Prasa Chief Executive by the DA when leaked reports showed roughly 190 contracts that were entered into between 2012 and 2016.

The DA's Manny De Freitas was quoted as saying, 'What's come through already from investigations by Treasury, is major corruption, maladministration, irregularities; and even Prasa's own regulations weren't met.' (449)

Alice VL

Alice VL

THE 'SAYINGS' OF TOP GOVERNMENT OFFICIALS

I am mortified. I am once more shown the ineptness of our government and the mindset that reigns over our beloved South Africa.

General Khehla John Sithola- National Police Commissioner

'If farm attacks really existed, we would know about them. I watch the news every day, but I don't hear of stories of farm attacks.' (450)

Co-operative Government and Traditional Affairs MEC—Nomusa Dube

'We will do an investigation and talk to the Department of Science and Technology on what is the cause of lightning. The Department has dealt with floods and fires, but lightning is new to us.' (451)

Ex-President—Jacob Zuma

'Even God expects us to rule this country because we are the only organization which was blessed by pastors when it was formed. It is even blessed in Heaven. That is why we will rule until Jesus comes back,' said Jacob Zuma in 2008. (452)

South African Sports Minister—Fikile Mbalula

'Last night we saw a bunch of losers — unbearable, useless individuals. We must never wake up to this. That mediocrity we saw yesterday is disgraceful. In Africa, we have won nothing — we are the laughing stock. This generation of players we must forget. It is back to the drawing board. The South African Football Association must draw up a detailed plan. They must wake up and smell the coffee,' said Fikile Mbalula. (453)

More from Ex-President Jacob Zuma:

'When I was in Venda recently I was so impressed to see how people there express respect for other people. A woman would clap her hands and even lie down to show respect. I was so impressed. If I was not already married to my wives I would go to Venda to look for a woman,' president Zuma stated. (454)

'This continent is the biggest continent in the world. All continents put together will fit into Africa,' he said while speaking to delegates at a World Economic Forum meeting. (455)

'(The ANC is) more important (than the constitution). (The constitution is only there) to regulate matters,' said the president while addressing delegates at a regional meeting. (456)

Alice VL

'A shower would minimize the risk of contracting the disease (HIV/AIDS).' (457)

Hlaudi Motsoeneng—Former South African Broadcasting Corporation (SABC) COO

'Your degrees don't work for you. You need experience to do the work. When these people come with their degrees, they drain the same people (who are skilled but don't have degrees.) (458)

'All that many educated people know how to do is to read the whole day. They don't have time to think. (459)

Collen Maine—ANC Youth League President

'I want actions to be taken so that the rand must fall. It must fall. We won't be dictated to by white monopoly capital.' (460)

Bathabile Dlamini—Minister of Social Development (Income R 2.M per year)

'These beneficiaries (of a pension of R 1,146.57) would have enough to buy adequate food as well as non-food items.' (461)

EFF leader Julius Malema: "There's no system that has worked successfully for Africans, except the Zimbabwean system." (462)

Alice VL

Former Health Minister—Manto Tshabalala-Msimang:

'Shall I repeat garlic, shall I talk about beetroot, shall I talk about lemon... these delay the development of HIV to Aids-defining conditions, and that's the truth.' (463)

Alice VL

CRY, MY BELOVED SOUTH AFRICA

The message is clear; there is no room in South Africa for the white, minority population. The ANC, the EFF, BFLF, IFP, and the ANC Government have been engaging in a silent, slow-building warfare against a targeted race, my race, in South Africa for years. Slow enough that the pursued South Africans, along with the world, doesn't notice, but quick enough to see the total extinction of the Afrikaner in South Africa within the next few years.

The South African Law has turned into the ANC law and is divided. Double standards are applied based on race as is evident in the many hate-speech charges and outcomes of late. When a group or race is specifically targeted for eradication, it must be labeled as genocide. *How can we not?* What else do we call it?

With the expropriation without compensation laws now frantically being altered and implemented, not only will many white South Africans find themselves without homes, but we will grow increasingly vulnerable and weakened by the threats to

Alice VL

eradicate us from South Africa.

Until my president acknowledges that farm attacks are soaring; until he admits that there is only a small percentage of jobs available to white South Africans, and until crimes are dealt with equally, white South Africans are now living in an apartheid-era of our own.

We live in prisons and hide from the world the moment the sun goes down. Bedrooms are secured, doors are locked, windows are protected, and every possible security measure available to us has been applied. Children no longer ride their bicycles outdoors or are free to engage in outdoor activities. Parks that have been taken over by criminals, and unsavory characters have now become a danger-zone for children.

Life in South Africa is demoralizing. Unnatural. South Africans are constantly exposed to scenes of universities, malls, schools, hospitals, municipal buildings, libraries, homes, and cars that are set alight and burnt down.

Racism is alive and well in South Africa. Violent protests are daily occurrences. Farm murders and home invasions are almost hourly occurrences. Hate-speech is on the increase and goes willfully 'undetected.'

Alice VL

Struggle songs calling for the murder of white South Africans are chanted daily. Threats are made against the minority South Africans to 'run back to the sea' or face a certain death.

Yet, daily mainstream news and media are criticizing these accounts as nothing more than white-driven-propaganda or white-supremacy.

How many slaughtered farmers must still be tortured and brutally murdered before the world notices?

How many white South Africans must still be discovered dead on their bedroom floors, in what is supposed to be the safety of their own homes, before the world notices?

How many children must still be drowned in boiling water, shot and stabbed before the world notices?

How high must the unemployment rate be before my president acknowledges that South Africans will eventually starve?

How many more police officers must be implicated in crimes such as cash-in-transit heists, robberies, farm murders and corruption before my president and understands that selected citizens are not protected?

Alice VL

How many more bribes must traffic officers accept before the world sees a problem?

How many old, fragile people must die in hospitals before the world yields to the incompetency of the employed South Africans?

How much crime must South African politicians, presidents, and cabinet members commit before the world sits up and notices?

When will the world ultimately relent and admit that genocide is currently taking place against the white, minority citizens of South Africa?

How can we find peace, harmony, and unity when we are a tribe, slaughtered for the color of our skin?

When will my turn come? Will I be murdered tonight, or will I have one more day to pray for my beloved South Africa?

Alice VL

INDEX

(1)https://www.iol.co.za/news/south-africa/northern-cape/piet-els-buried-on-his-farm-15082941
(2)https://citizen.co.za/news/south-africa/1033566/randfontein-massacre-victim-remembered/
(3) https://www.youtube.com/watch?v=eFqIv7tQ0nA
(4) https://www.bbc.com/news/world-africa-45026931
(5)https://www.rt.com/business/419543-south-africa-land-compensation-whites/
(6)https://www.scribd.com/doc/284112299/650-PAGE-list-of-names-of-murdered-white-people-in-South-Africa
(7) https://www.youtube.com/watch?v=AOaLlIxxQlQ
(8) https://www.youtube.com/watch?v=pl5QYjh0EJs
(9) https://www.youtube.com/watch?v=nL9eXc1hP8A
(10) https://www.youtube.com/watch?v=S8mMA4ptzcU
(11) https://www.youtube.com/watch?v=nWhXzS0ZRa8
(12) https://www.youtube.com/watch?v=8Dg5247UpjA
(13) https://www.youtube.com/watch?v=hWgKkw1mWDs
(14) https://www.youtube.com/watch?v=6vjb0w67PZ8
(15) https://www.youtube.com/watch?v=K9vUZ20MIr4
(16) https://www.youtube.com/watch?v=mkfU3fmsvfo
(17) https://www.youtube.com/watch?v=y6LYmMl0Nig
(18) https://www.youtube.com/watch?v=XVd-_cZILhA
(19) https://www.youtube.com/watch?v=vs4USzKIGoU
(20) https://www.youtube.com/watch?v=kmuAbKJH9XM
(21) https://www.youtube.com/watch?v=PUJQAVSnlV4
(22) https://www.youtube.com/watch?v=FEq5nduxZCA
(23)https://www.iol.co.za/news/politics/anti-jewish-andilemngxitama-rages-on-10946632
(24)https://www.thesouthafrican.com/australia-fast-track-visa-south-african-farmers/
(25)   https://www.rt.com/business/432375-russia-south-africa-farmers/

Alice VL

(26)https://southafricatoday.net/south-africa-news/protest-march-against-attacks-on-whites-and-farmers-auckland-new-zealand/
(27)https://www.newsweek.com/world-south-africa-south-african-farmers-australia-845534
(28)https://ewn.co.za/2018/03/16/sisulu-issues-diplomatic-demarche-to-australia-over-white-sa-farmers-visas
(29)https://www.news24.com/SouthAfrica/News/beneficiaries-of-colonialism-will-be-defeated-in-sa-ancwl-to-uk-mep-20180302
(30)   https://www.rt.com/business/432375-russia-south-africa-farmers/
(31)   https://www.wikigender.org/wiki/ages-of-consent-to-sex-in-south-africa/ (Act 32 of 2007)
(32)https://www.mirror.co.uk/3am/celebrity-news/katie-hopkins-detained-south-africa-11977548
(33) https://www.youtube.com/watch?v=a_bDc7FfItk
(34)https://newsoweto.co.za/saps-refer-farm-attacks-house-ordinary-robbery-mngxitama-says-farm-murders-black-revenge/
(35)https://www.dailymaverick.co.za/article/2014-02-26-dysfunctional-detective-units-disappearing-dockets-and-a-dereliction-of-duty-meet-khayelitshas-police/
(36)https://newsoweto.co.za/leaked-document-anc-kill-boer-kill-farmer-plot-since-1993-must-read/
(37)https://www.suidlanders.co.za/the-right-to-self-preservation-sa-prepper/
(38)http://www.pressreader.com/south-africa/cape-times/20171219/281479276772087
(39)https://external-preview.redd.it/mQm3UtbC1HL8MJjmBqzi5hrJURX8vq8ZXvj04byWh6o.jpg?auto=webp&s=c80f0b89df52bfc1623ef1776d2d2a3ee7c18089
(40) https://walkers.co.za/racial-quota-systems/
(41) http://www.safrpsa.org/our-mission.html
(42)https://www.theguardian.com/media/2017/sep/05/bell-pottingersouth-africa-pr-firm
(43)https://www.timeslive.co.za/news/south-africa/2017-09-04-the-guptas-bell-pottinger-and-the-fake-news-propaganda-machine/
(44)https://www.timeslive.co.za/news/south-africa/2017-06-23-south-africans-beat-bell-pottinger-at-its-own-twitter-game/
(45)https://www.businesslive.co.za/bd/national/2018-08-23-stay-out-of-sas-affairs-julius-malema-warns-donald-trump/

Alice VL

(46)http://www.uncapturedsa.co.za/10_stages_of_GENOCIDE_and_S
A_at_stage_6&p=read&aid=125
(47)http://genocidewatch.net/about-us-2/articles-by-dr-gregory-
stanton/
(48) http://www.pbs.org/pov/promisedland/background/
(54)https://www.brandsouthafrica.com/investments-
immigration/business/trends/empowerment/black-economic-
empowerment-codes-of-good-practice
(55)https://web.archive.org/web/20070927200634/http://www.dti.g
ov.za/bee/beecodes.htm
(56)https://mywage.co.za/decent-work/fair-treatment/affirmative-
action
(40)https://www.theguardian.com/tv-and-
radio/tvandradioblog/2010/may/13/zimbabwe-robert-mugabe-land-
reform
(48)https://www.theguardian.com/uk-news/2017/jul/10/bell-
pottinger-pr-firm-apologizes-south-africa-campaign
 (49)https://www.telegraph.co.uk/news/2017/02/28/husband-
woman-tortured-south-africa-robbery-speaks-horrific/
(50)https://www.news24.com/SouthAfrica/News/robbers-tortured-
woman-with-drill-in-farm-attack-20170311
 (51)https://www.news24.com/SouthAfrica/News/Grisly-farm-
murder-scene-indescribable-20110210
(52)http://censorbugbear-reports.blogspot.com/2011/05/shot-
ottosdal-farmer-dragged-15km.html
(53)https://www.news24.com/SouthAfrica/News/Grim-details-of-
Lindley-murders-emerge-20110525
(54)https://www.theguardian.com/world/2003/sep/26/southafrica.ro
rycarroll1
(55)http://www.dailymail.co.uk/news/article-2179171/Walkerville-
family-murders-Horrific-death-boy-12-drowned-boiling-water-
robbers-raped-mother.html
(56)   http://censorbugbear-reports.blogspot.com/2010/06/boer-
womans-womb-carved-from-her-body.html
(57)https://www.iol.co.za/news/victim-tells-of-brutal-farm-attack-
1695721
(58) https://southafricatoday.net/tag/elizabeth-kotze/
(59)https://www.iol.co.za/news/south-africa/farm-murder-described-
as-gruesome-484216

Alice VL

(60)https://citizen.co.za/news/news-cns/1897129/woman-dies-during-south-cape-farm-attack/
(61)https://southafricatoday.net/south-africa-news/north-west/brutal-farm-attack-man-very-seriously-harmed-kuilfontein/
(62)   https://krugersdorpnews.co.za/359826/just-in-police-confirm-farm-attack-on-two-70-year-olds/
(63)   https://southafricatoday.net/south-africa-news/western-cape/farm-attack-alert-farmer-fires-on-attackers-saves-family-paarl/
(64)https://southafricatoday.net/south-africa-news/mpumalanga/farm-attack-elderly-couple-and-grandson-overpowered-wakkerstroom/
(65)https://www.pressreader.com/south-africa/the-herald-south-africa/20180605/281689730501154
(66)https://www.news24.com/SouthAfrica/News/Farmer-beaten-tied-to-tree-then-shot-20120131
(67)https://southafricatoday.net/south-africa-news/free-state/farm-murder-woman-74-severely-assaulted-and-raped-reitz-fs/
(68)   https://www.sabreakingnews.co.za/2018/03/23/survivor-describes-how-close-friend-died-in-brutal-farm-attack/
(69)http://freewestmedia.com/2018/03/25/human-rights-day-sees-jasper-von-kleist-killed-on-farm/
(70)https://www.iol.co.za/news/farm-couple-killed-a-month-apart-1439077
(71)https://southafricatoday.net/south-africa-news/free-state/farmer-71-shot-dead-robbed-vredefort/
(72)https://www.timeslive.co.za/news/south-africa/2017-12-19-eastern-cape-farmer-dies-weeks-after-brutal-attack/
(73) https://nari.co.za/d.php?fid=14927
(74)https://www.enca.com/south-africa/teen-shattered-after-parents-grandparents-murdered-on-farm
(75)https://southafricatoday.net/south-africa-news/gauteng/farm-attack-manager-critical-after-being-shot-in-the-head-lanseria/
(76)https://southafricatoday.net/south-africa-news/gauteng/farm-attack-young-man-shot-in-the-chest-cullinan/
(77)https://southafricatoday.net/south-africa-news/limpopo/fram-attack-couple-tied-up-assaulted-vehicle-look-out-boshoek/
(78)https://southafricatoday.net/south-africa-news/gauteng/farm-attack-woman-stabbed-in-hand-with-screwdriver-mooiplaats/
(79)https://southafricatoday.net/south-africa-news/north-

west/bokfontein-farm-attack-couple-tied-up-hacked-with-panga/
(80)https://southafricatoday.net/south-africa-news/van-stadensrus-
farm-murders-were-brutal-execution-style-slayings/
(81)https://southafricatoday.net/south-africa-news/van-stadensrus-
farm-murders-were-brutal-execution-style-slayings/
(82)https://www.arrivealive.co.za/news.aspx?i=34923&s=0&page=Ma
n-stabbed-and-killed-in-alleged-robbery-on-a-farm-on-the-corner-of-
the-R44-and-Annandale-road-in-Stellenbosch
(83)https://www.timeslive.co.za/news/south-africa/2018-06-24-
stellenbosch-farmer-jeffrey-zetler-was-killed-in-robbery-police/
(84)https://rekordnorth.co.za/130256/newsflash-man-shot-pta-north-
farm-attack/
(85)https://southafricatoday.net/south-africa-news/limpopo/farm-
attack-woman-85-overpowered-assaulted-duiwelskloof/
(86)https://www.news24.com/SouthAfrica/News/man-fatally-shot-
woman-injured-in-komatipoort-farm-attack-20180617
(87) https://nari.co.za/d.php?fid=13258
(88)https://southafricatoday.net/south-africa-news/free-state/farm-
murder-woman-74-severely-assaulted-and-raped-reitz-fs/
(89)https://southafricatoday.net/south-africa-news/free-state/farm-
attack-couple-admitted-to-hospital-reitz-fs/
(90)https://www.news24.com/SouthAfrica/News/man-involved-in-
limpopo-farm-attack-arrested-20180602
(91)https://southafricatoday.net/south-africa-news/gauteng/man-
shot-dead-in-farm-attack-hillside-randfontein/
(92)https://southafricatoday.net/south-africa-news/eastern-
cape/farm-attack-elderly-couple-tied-up-robbed-pe/
(93)https://southafricatoday.net/south-africa-
news/gauteng/gruesome-mothers-day-farm-murders-1-suspect-
arrested-1-sought/
(94)https://southafricatoday.net/south-africa-news/limpopo/farm-
attack-couple-injured-two-vehicles-look-out-bela-bela/
(95)http://www.zobo.co.za/news/farm-attack-man-admitted-to-
hospital-rustenburg#.W60T9mhKhhE
(96)https://lowvelder.co.za/396575/victim-of-farm-attack-passes-in-
hospital/
(97)http://newsupdatessa.site/farm-attack-cash-four-firearms-
jewelry-and-other-household-items-two-vehicles-stolen-in-farm-
attack-please-assist-to-locate/

Alice VL

(98)https://southafricatoday.net/south-africa-news/kwazulu-natal/elandslaagte-farm-attack-workers-tied-up-firearms-stolen/
(99)https://southafricatoday.net/south-africa-news/mpumalanga/farm-worker-seriously-injured-in-panga-attack-ogies/
(100)http://newsupdatessa.site/terrorists-attack-farm-assault-tie-up-wife-ad-workers-kroonstad/
(101)https://southafricatoday.net/south-africa-news/limpopo/farm-workers-tied-up-manager-attacked-with-panga-rankins-pass/
(102)https://southafricatoday.net/south-africa-news/free-state/panga-attack-on-a-farm-elderly-couple-seriously-injured-hertzogville/
(103)https://southafricatoday.net/south-africa-news/gauteng/savage-farm-attack-victim-starting-to-stabilize-sunrella/
(104)https://southafricatoday.net/south-africa-news/north-west/farm-attack-woman-60-brutally-attacked-hospitalised-vryburg/
(105)https://southafricatoday.net/south-africa-news/north-west/rustenburg-farm-attack-traumatised-family-assaulted-tied-with-wire/
(106)https://southafricatoday.net/south-africa-news/kwazulu-natal/farmers-wife-dies-in-brutal-savage-attack-umhlali/
(107) https://www.iol.co.za/news/south-africa/northern-cape/couple-in-hospital-after-farm-attack-14531030
(108)https://southafricatoday.net/south-africa-news/eastern-cape/farmer-shot-and-killed-outside-his-farm-peelton-ec/
(109) https://southafricatoday.net/south-africa-news/north-west/brutal-farm-attack-mom-and-young-children-savagely-beaten-bokfontein/
(110)https://southafricatoday.net/south-africa-news/north-west/farm-attack-four-men-tied-up-and-stabbed-brits/
(111)https://southafricatoday.net/south-africa-news/eastern-cape/violent-joubertina-farm-attack-second-suspect-arrested/
(112) https://southafricatoday.net/south-africa-news/free-state/farmer-80-brutally-stabbed-assaulted-and-interrogated-paul-roux/
(113)https://southafricatoday.net/south-africa-news/kwazulu-natal/farm-attack-man-ambushed-and-severely-beaten-franklin/
(114)https://southafricatoday.net/south-africa-news/eastern-cape/farmers-wife-shot-raped-in-front-of-wire-tied-children-hackney/

Alice VL

(115)https://southafricatoday.net/south-africa-news/eastern-cape/elderly-family-members-tied-up-bludgeoned-bushy-park-smallholding/

(116)https://southafricatoday.net/south-africa-news/free-state/farmer-tied-upside-down-hacked-to-death-wife-raped-ladybrand/

(117)https://southafricatoday.net/south-africa-news/western-cape/farmer-stabbed-to-death-in-attack-tulbagh/

(118)   https://southafricatoday.net/south-africa-news/western-cape/farm-attack-woman-62-assaulted-tied-up-moorreesburg/

(119) https://southafricatoday.net/south-africa-news/gauteng/family-of-six-attacked-tied-up-on-smallholding-knoppieslaagte/

(120)https://southafricatoday.net/south-africa-news/northern-cape/woman-65-brutally-murdered-smallholding-grobelershoop/

(121)   https://southafricatoday.net/south-africa-news/mpumalanga/farm-attack-woman-72-found-tied-up-and-murdered-chrissiesmeer/

(122)   https://southafricatoday.net/south-africa-news/north-west/farmer-severely-assaulted-in-attack-hospitalized-lichtenburg/

(123)https://www.news24.com/SouthAfrica/News/hunt-on-for-murderers-involved-in-secunda-farm-attack-20180217

 (124)https://southafricatoday.net/south-africa-news/northern-cape/farm-attack-farmer-82-and-wife-hospitalized-windsorton/

(125)https://archive.org/stream/guideforzulucour00rudoiala#page/20/mode/2up

(126) https://southafricatoday.net/south-africa-news/free-state/man-76-violently-assaulted-in-farm-attack-reitz-fs/

 (127)https://southafricatoday.net/south-africa-news/limpopo/man-lucky-to-be-alive-after-farm-attack-melkrivier/

(128) ttps://www.arrivealive.co.za/news.aspx?s=1&i=33652&page=Gauteng-Farm-attack-in-Hekpoort-Gauteng

(129)https://southafricatoday.net/south-africa-news/limpopo/harrowing-story-2nd-farm-attack-wife-kills-intruder-groblersdal/

(130)   https://southafricatoday.net/south-africa-news/eastern-cape/farm-uitijk-elderly-couple-attacked-by-4-armed-men-aliwal-north/

Alice VL

(131)https://southafricatoday.net/south-africa-news/gauteng/farm-attack-man-and-wife-shot-and-robbed-muldersdrift/
(132)   https://southafricatoday.net/south-africa-news/north-west/farmer-critical-in-icu-after-attack-on-his-farm-broederstroom/
(133)https://southafricatoday.net/south-africa-news/north-west/farm-attack-33-farmer-hospitalized-vryburg/
(134)https://southafricatoday.net/south-africa-news/mpumalanga/farmers-house-burned-down-after-robbery/
(135)https://www.rnews.co.za/article/17947/elderly-grahamstown-retirees-attacked-in-their-home-two-suspects-arrested-on-the-scene
(136)https://southafricatoday.net/south-africa-news/western-cape/farmer-and-son-stabbed-in-farm-attack/
(137)https://southafricatoday.net/south-africa-news/gauteng/nooitgedacht-home-invasion-man-shot-dead-in-front-of-his-wife/
(138)https://www.afriforum.co.za/police-minister-denies-farm-murders-not-declaring-priority-crimes/
(139)https://www.facebook.com/1114495942042590/photos/whites-should-go-and-bury-their-loved-ones-overseas-where-they-came-from-says-la/1116797955145722/
(140)https://southafricalatest.com/2018/07/25/whites-should-go-and-bury-their-loved-ones-overseas-where-they-came-from-says-land-affairs-minister-maite-nkoana-mashabane/
(141)www.news24.com/SouthAfrica-to-usit-was-stolen-from-us-mngxitama-20170719
(142)https://dailycaller.com/2018/08/30/south-africa-white-farms-white-farmers/

(143) https://www.youtube.com/watch?v=cHLTKZ05zM4
(144)https://www.telegraph.co.uk/news/worldnews/africaandindiano cean/southafrica/9716539/South-African-farmers-fearing-for-their-lives.html
(145)https://mg.co.za/article/2017-10-30-south-africas-farm-murder-statistics-are-more-political-than-accurate
(146) https://issafrica.org/author/johan-burger
(147) https://www.youtube.com/watch?v=2-cB73jXoYc
(148)https://southafricangenocide.com/farmmurderscarte-blanche-directly-links-julius-malema-to-farm-murders-video/
(149https://www.iol.co.za/dailynews/news/read-mans-detailed-plans-

for-chatsworth-robbery-15970754
(150)http://mantissecurity.co.za/home-invasion-south-africa-mantis-security-wants-you-to-know-these-top-facts-about-local-intrusions/
(151)https://rekordcenturion.co.za/18280/watch-out-for-house-break-in-markings/
(152)   https://www.iol.co.za/news/cops-warn-of-signs-left-by-criminals-1766937
(153) http://www.loc.gov/law/help/firearms-control/southafrica.php
(154)https://www.timeslive.co.za/news/south-africa/2018-06-07-end-of-the-road-for-firearm-owners-who-fail-to-renew-licences-on-time/
(155)https://www.news24.com/Columnists/GuestColumn/unfair-allocation-of-police-resources-reinforces-social-inequality-20180720
(156)https://www.thesouthafrican.com/home-invasions-defending-myself/
(157)https://www.news24.com/SouthAfrica/News/robbers-kill-north-west-man-who-tried-to-protect-his-daughter-20180624
(158)https://www.news24.com/SouthAfrica/Local/South-Coast-Fever/pensioner-attacked-at-retirement-village-20180526
(159)https://www.news24.com/SouthAfrica/Local/South-Coast-Fever/pensioner-attacked-at-retirement-village-20180526
(160)https://www.news24.com/SouthAfrica/News/murdered-bloch-couple-to-be-honoured-at-memorial-service-20180515
(161)https://www.all4women.co.za/1417963/news/south-african-news/businesswoman-shot-home-forced-car-taken-atm-robber
(162)https://www.timeslive.co.za/news/south-africa/2018-03-16-jeweller-fighting-for-his-life-after-deadly-home-invasion/
(163)https://www.dailysun.co.za/News/National/former-policeman-shot-dead-in-robbery-20180225
(164)https://www.news24.com/SouthAfrica/News/more-questions-than-answers-after-cape-town-shooting-leaves-3-children-man-dead-20180404
(165)https://www.news24.com/SouthAfrica/News/poverty-no-excuse-for-robbing-raping-and-murdering-franziska-judge-20170607
(166)https://www.news24.com/SouthAfrica/News/murdered-maties-student-apparently-also-raped-20170529
(167)https://www.news24.com/SouthAfrica/News/brutally-murdered-kzn-mans-face-unrecognisable-20171031
(168)https://www.iol.co.za/news/south-africa/gauteng/81-year-old-cleric-in-icu-after-thugs-brutal-assault-15992006

Alice VL

(169)https://southafricatoday.net/south-africa-news/86-year-old-woman-severely-assaulted-in-house-robbery/
(170)https://rekordeast.co.za/175177/newsflash-pretoria-east-man-46-found-dead-garden/
(171) https://southafricatoday.net/tag/dillon-barnard/
(172)https://citizen.co.za/news/south-africa/1973765/elderly-woman-allegedly-murdered-at-mbombela-care-centre/
(173)http://www.hinnews.com/za/metro-news/heart-bleeding-ann-smit-86-found-lying-in-a-pool-of-blood-in-her-house-port-elizabeth
(174)https://southafricatoday.net/south-africa-news/gauteng/frail-man-82-simply-slaughtered-in-his-home-garsfontein/
(175)http://www.joydigitalmag.com/news/retired-reverend-kicked-beaten-hands-tied-behind-back/
(176)https://southafricatoday.net/south-africa-news/north-west/shell-garage-owner-fatally-shot-father-assaulted-leeudoringstad/
(177)https://www.news24.com/SouthAfrica/News/daughter-of-man-killed-in-broederstroom-armed-robbery-we-should-fight-back-20180702
(178)https://www.thesouthafrican.com/sona2018-read-the-full-text-of-cyril-ramaphosas-address-here/
(179)https://www.independent.co.uk/news/world/africa/south-africa-white-farms-land-seizure-anc-race-relations-a8234461.html
(180)https://www.biznews.com/africa/2017/12/27/ethnic-hatred-sa-farm-murders-herbst
(181) http://praag.org/?p=20612
(182)https://www.moneyweb.co.za/news/south-africa/sa-expropriation-plan-to-exclude-black-owned-land/
(183)http://www.politicsweb.co.za/politics/land-expropriation-aimed-at-whites--pieter-groenew
(184)https://www.pressreader.com/south-africa/the-sunday-independent/20180708/281612421159285
(185)https://www.jacarandafm.com/news/news/ramaphosa-there-will-be-no-smash-and-grab-land/
(186)https://www.iol.co.za/news/politics/acdp-ramaphosas-denial-of-land-grabs-farm-murders-deeply-disappointing-17274600
(187)https://www.hrw.org/report/2002/03/08/fast-track-land-reform-zimbabwe
(188)https://www.express.co.uk/news/world/1006892/south-africa-

land-seizure-white-farmers-land-grab-ANC-expropriation-
compensation-cyril-ram
(189)https://www.timeslive.co.za/news/south-africa/2018-03-27-
tragic-consequences-of-land-grab-in-hermanus/
(190)https://www.sapeople.com/2018/07/14/owners-pay-mortgages-
while-homes-hijacked-by-thugs-in-south-africa-coming-up-on-cb/
(191)https://www.thesouthafrican.com/farmer-charged-with-
attempted-murder-after-firing-paintball-gun-at-intruder/
(192)https://www.groundup.org.za/article/hundreds-flock-occupy-
municipal-land-pietermaritzburg/
(193)https://www.timeslive.co.za/news/south-africa/2018-06-01-
land-occupiers-set-building-alight-with-family-inside/
(194)https://www.iol.co.za/dailynews/pics-farms-burnt-as-violent-
protests-erupt-in-kzn-13832929
(195)http://www.dailymail.co.uk/news/article-6094565/White-
farmer-set-game-reserve-seized-South-Africa-calls-theft.html
(196)https://www.thesouthafrican.com/marikana-what-did-cyril-
ramaphosa-do/
(197)http://venturesafrica.com/south-africas-top-five-bee-wealthiest-
individuals/
(198)https://www.sahistory.org.za/dated-event/steve-hofmeyer-sa-
singer-born
(199) Mense Van My Asem (Steve Hofmeyr bio)
(200)https://www.huffingtonpost.co.za/2017/10/03/steve-hofmeyr-
rants-about-wrong-farm-murder-statistics_a_23230729/
(201) https://www.facebook.com/Steve.Hofmeyr/
(202)https://www.thesouthafrican.com/blacks-were-the-architects-of-
apartheid-tweet-deals-heavy-blow-to-afrikaans-culture-can-we-
blame-steve-now/
(203)https://okmzansi.co.za/can-trace-roots-back-sa-julius-malema-
says-steve-hofmeyr/
(204)https://www.sowetanlive.co.za/news/2010-12-07-hofmeyr-
under-fire-over-racist-rant/
(205)https://www.news24.com/SouthAfrica/News/Farm-murderers-
leave-chilling-note-20101203
(206)https://www.news24.com/SouthAfrica/News/Grim-details-of-
Lindley-murders-emerge-20110525
(207)http://censorbugbear-reports.blogspot.com/2010/12/more-
death-threats-for-steve-hofmeyr.html

Alice VL

(208)http://censorbugbear-reports.blogspot.com/2010/12/death-threats-target-afrikaans-singer.html
(209)https://www.timeslive.co.za/sunday-times/lifestyle/2015-06-07-is-steve-hofmeyr-really-as-racist-as-he-seems/
(210)https://www.thesouthafrican.com/steve-hofmeyrs-new-zealand-concert-cancelled-after-uproar/
(211)http://www.african-european.com/2017/01/13/international-protest-launched-nederburg-to-allow-extreme-rightwing-singer-steve-hofmeyr/
(212)https://www.enca.com/south-africa/die-stem-song-oppressors-racists-and-mass-murderers-eff
(213)https://mg.co.za/article/2015-03-17-pick-n-pay-landrover-pull-out-of-afrikaans-is-groot-concerts
(214)https://www.news24.com/SouthAfrica/News/Another-Afrikaans-music-festival-shunsHofmeyr-20150201
(215)http://www.2oceansvibe.com/2015/02/02/the-walls-are-closing-in-on-steve-hofmeyr/
(216)ttps://www.flatinternational.org/template_volume.php?volume_id=272
(217)http://www.2oceansvibe.com/2016/06/01/blind-netherlands-restaurant-cancels-steve-hofmeyr-gig-because-he-is-a-white-supremacist/
(218)https://www.news24.com/SouthAfrica/News/steve-hofmeyr-talk-at-ct-press-club-cancelled-20161013
(219)https://www.facebook.com/Steve.Hofmeyr/posts/die-volledige-persklubtoespraak-in-english-as-agreedin-die-noorde-het-ons-n-gebo/10154654137169559/
(220)https://www.facebook.com/Steve.Hofmeyr/posts/10156550885209559
(221)www.municipaliq.co.za/publications/press/201807110947026629.doc
(222)https://www.news24.com/SouthAfrica/News/kzn-library-torched-during-service-delivery-protests-20180709
(223)https://ewn.co.za/2018/07/16/call-for-the-army-to-be-deployed-to-protest-stricken-zwelihle
(224)https://ewn.co.za/2018/07/14/police-disperse-crowd-of-protesters-in-midrand
(225) https://www.kimberley.org.za/tag/service-delivery-protests/
(226)https://ewn.co.za/2018/05/08/police-fire-rubber-bullets-to-

disperse-protesters-in-olievenhoutbosch

(227)https://www.news24.com/SouthAfrica/News/bottoms-out-anc-women-bare-bums-in-tshwane-protest-20160119

(228)https://www.news24.com/SouthAfrica/News/4-houses-burnt-in-renewed-coligny-protests-20170508

(229)https://southafricatoday.net/media/south-africa-video/protest-videos/riots-this-is-whats-left-at-embalenhle-mall-secunda/

(230)https://citizen.co.za/news/1953577/plettenberg-bay-a-war-zone-say-residents/

(231)https://www.enca.com/south-africa/watch-cape-town-shop-owners-flee-from-looting-protesters

(232)https://www.timeslive.co.za/news/south-africa/2018-06-12-riebeek-kasteel-tense-after-violent-protests/

(233)https://ewn.co.za/2018/01/17/parent-assaulted-as-eff-members-protest-outside-vereeniging-school

(234)https://businesstech.co.za/news/government/138169/damage-to-sa-universities-hits-r600-million-and-counting/

(235)https://www.news24.com/SouthAfrica/News/dept-explains-why-23-vuwani-schools-have-still-not-been-repaired-20180504

(236)   https://www.news24.com/SouthAfrica/News/ukzn-src-condemns-burning-of-law-library-20160907

(237)https://www.iol.co.za/news/south-africa/144-service-delivery-protests-recorded-in-2018-so-far-15961274

(238)   https://citizen.co.za/news/south-africa/1965631/watch-the-burnt-remains-of-looted-mpumalanga-mall/

(239) https://www.youtube.com/watch?v=qNWHT7k8F-k

(240)https://www.independent.co.uk/news/world/africa/south-africa-white-farmers-eff-mbuyiseni-ndlozi-anc-interview-a8271096.html

(241)   https://blf.org.za/2018/03/15/whites-must-go-back-to-europe-not-australia/

(242)https://www.news24.com/SouthAfrica/News/vicki-momberg-sentenced-to-an-effective-2-years-in-prison-for-racist-rant-20180328

(243)https://www.thesouthafrican.com/white-people-sandf-majors-racist-comments/

(244)https://www.thesouthafrican.com/sandf-major-fired-comments-white-people/

(245)https://www.reuters.com/article/us-safrica-racism/south-african-woman-jailed-in-landmark-ruling-for-racist-rant-idUSKBN1H42DA

Alice VL

(246)https://me.me/i/i-reported-this-facebook-comment-yesterday-jama-sethu-jaceni-please-a273cac4e1e946f68f6615eef9327ca2
(247)https://twitter.com/theerimtanangle/status/1010096039708147712?lang=en
(248)https://www.news24.com/SouthAfrica/News/Malema-blamed-for-farm-attack-20100315
(249) https://www.youtube.com/watch?v=6vjb0w67PZ8
(250)www.onlinedebate.net › ... › The Club House › Member Contributed News
(251)https://www.timeslive.co.za/politics/2011-09-12-malema-guilty-of-hate-speech/
(252) http://www.genocidewatch.org/southafrica.html
(253)https://www.thesouthafrican.com/blf-kill-the-boer-one-settler-one-bullet/
(254)https://www.timeslive.co.za/politics/2018-08-23-malema-tells-pathological-liar-trump-to-keep-nose-out-affairs-in-sa/
(255)https://www.news24.com/SouthAfrica/News/was-the-assault-rifle-malema-fired-an-ak-47-20180801
(256)https://citizen.co.za/news/south-africa/1966767/malema-says-he-is-maybe-behind-farm-murders/
(257)https://www.huffingtonpost.co.za/2018/06/12/malema-we-have-not-called-for-the-killing-of-white-people-at-least-for-now_a_23456601/
(258) https://www.sahistory.org.za/people/julius-sello-malema
(259)http://www.politicsweb.co.za/archive/afriforum-lays-corruption-charges-against-julius-m
(260)   http://censorbugbear-reports.blogspot.com/2009/12/death-threats-against-sa-whites-on.html
(261)http://censorbugbear-reports.blogspot.com/2010/12/i-must-kill-this-devil-settler-sabelo.html
(262)http://www.ilanamercer.com/phprunner/public_article_list_view.php?editid1=544
(263)https://southafricatoday.net/south-africa-news/eastern-cape/why-is-mveleli-mogolwane-gwabeni-still-in-service/
(264)https://me.me/i/mampuru-mampuru-we-need-to-unite-as-black-people-there-21621332
(265)https://www.facebook.com/AltAfrikaner/posts/not-so-hard-to-work/1633059086730643/
(266)

https://twitter.com/onlinemagazin/status/977597335143436288
(267)https://www.huffingtonpost.co.za/2018/04/03/clean-sa-of-whites-social-media-post-case-heads-to-equality-court_a_23401381/
(268)http://www.politicsweb.co.za/news-and-analysis/whites-deserve-to-be-hacked-and-killed-like-jews--
(269)https://www.huffingtonpost.co.za/2018/07/09/malema-causes-stir-with-violence-against-whites-video-tweet_a_23477467/
(270)https://www.thesouthafrican.com/violence-against-whites-julius-malema-tweets-in-agreement/
(271) https://waisworld.org/go.jsp?id=02a&o=119514
(272)https://dailykenn.blogspot.com/2018/05/extremists-want-to-exclude-colonial.html
(273)https://www.timeslive.co.za/politics/2018-07-18-blf-in-equality-court-for-hate-speech/
(274)http://www.sajr.co.za/news-and-articles/2017/09/07/andile-faces-equality-court-over-hate-tweets
(275)https://www.gettyimages.com/detail/news-photo/members-of-political-party-black-first-land-first-wear-news-photo/855139848
(276) https://www.youtube.com/watch?v=aqx-HxIfeKY
(277)https://www.news24.com/Archives/City-Press/An-ideal-to-die-for-20150429
(278)https://www.afriforum.co.za/afriforum-lays-criminal-charges-regarding-racist-attacks-social-media/
(279)http://www.polity.org.za/article/afriforum-lays-criminal-charges-against-police-officials-2018-06-18
(280)https://southafricatoday.net/south-africa-news/kwazulu-natal/blf-spews-out-hatred-applauds-attack-on-white-eshowe-farm/
(281)http://www.politicsweb.co.za/documents/how-the-response-to-black-and-white-racism-differs
(286)https://www.sahistory.org.za/article/history-apartheid-south-africa
(287) https://www.urbandictionary.com/define.php?term=k (5)
(288)https://www.expatica.com/za/about/Social-security-in-South-Africa_105901.html
(289)http://www.wecanchange.co.za/Editors/Articles/tabid/55/itemid/2141/amid/376/sassa-grant-fraud-r800-million-lost-to-corruption.aspx
(290)http://www.hrpulse.co.za/news/233966-cps-officials-identified-in-sassa-fraud-syndicate

Alice VL

(291)https://ewn.co.za/2016/05/27/14-members-of-social-grant-fraud-syndicate-arrested
(297)http://content.time.com/time/magazine/article/0,9171,145854,00.html
(298)   http://afrikanervolksparty.org/index.php/media/160-artikels/5100-opening-pandoras-apartheid-box-part-11.html?lang=af
(299) https://www.news24.com/southafrica/news/volksraad-hits-out-at-afrikaans-media-20111003
(300)https://southafricatoday.net/south-africa-news/gauteng/whites-chased-from-shopping-mall-by-eff-thugs-centurion/
(281)https://www.cnn.com/2018/02/16/africa/south-africa-politics-intl/index.html
(282)https://www.businesslive.co.za/bd/national/2018-03-02-gugile-nkwinti-all-land-going-back-to-1652-must-be-returned-to-the-people/
(283)https://www.businesslive.co.za/bd/national/2018-03-02-julius-malema-the-time-for-reconciliation-is-over-now-is-the-time-for-justice/
(284)https://twitter.com/hatecrimesa/status/950798611843076096?lang=bg
(285)   https://www.iol.co.za/news/south-africa/gauteng/woman-accuses-restaurant-owners-of-racism-8094128
(286)https://twitter.com/the_war_economy/status/1001539426982551557
(287)https://southafricatoday.net/south-africa-news/white-man-you-stole-the-land-malema/
(288)https://www.farmersweekly.co.za/agri-news/south-africa/land-audit-provides-new-figures-ownership/
(289) https://academic.oup.com/mbe/article/26/7/1581/1123707
(290)http://www.sahistory.org.za/dated-event/smallpox-epidemic-strikes-cape
(291) https://www.ncbi.nlm.nih.gov/pmc/articles/PMC1288201/
(292)http://www.capetowndiamondmuseum.org/about-diamonds/south-african-diamond-history/
(293)https://showme.co.za/facts-about-south-africa/history-of-south-africa/the-history-of-south-africa/
(294)https://www.businessinsider.co.za/protection-of-investment-act-commencement-gazetted-foreign-mediation-bee-section-25-constitution-2018-7
(295)https://businesstech.co.za/news/government/61393/sa-

government-offering-incentives-to-keep-whites-out-of-jobs/
(296)http://www.abc.net.au/news/2016-08-01/white-south-africans-
complain-of-a-reverse-apartheid/7676764
(297)https://thegrapevine.theroot.com/cry-me-a-river-of-white-tears-
white-south-african-colo-1823331790
(298) https://southafricatoday.net/south-africa-news/white-people-
now-finally-excluded-from-the-south-african-job-market/
(299)https://www.dailymail.co.uk/news/article-3462336/The-white-
squatter-camps-South-Africa-home-hundreds-families-enduring-
terrible-poverty-blame-fall-Apartheid.html
(300)https://www.iol.co.za/news/politics/thumamina-people-are-
tired-of-businesses-being-run-by-a-minority-15885817
(301)https://www.timeslive.co.za/news/south-africa/2018-09-02-
solidarity-plan-strategic-strike-at-sasol-over-share-scheme-that-
excludes-white-staff/
(302)https://www.facebook.com/WoolworthsSA/posts/over-the-past-
few-days-weve-been-accused-of-racist-employment-practices-wed-
like/10151066154653178/
(303)https://www.iol.co.za/news/politics/pallo-jordan-has-no-
qualifications-report-1729673
(304)https://www.news24.com/SouthAfrica/News/i-educated-myself-
zuma-tells-pupils-20160722
(305)https://www.news24.com/SouthAfrica/News/Degree-mills-
continue-to-provide-fake-academic-qualifications-20150908
(306)https://www.news24.com/Archives/City-Press/How-Hlaudi-
Motsoeneng-lied-in-SABC-application-4-Es-and-an-F-in-matric-
20150429
(307)https://www.news24.com/Archives/City-Press/Pallo-Jordans-
wisdom-not-confined-to-degrees-Stone-Sizani-20150429
(308)https://www.corruptionwatch.org.za/time-to-stop-the-rot-at-
the-sabc/
(309)https://mybroadband.co.za/news/government/107960-sa-
presidents-qualifications-1989-to-2014.html
(310)https://www.news24.com/Drum/Archive/your-degrees-cant-
work-for-you-sabc-boss-motsoeneng-20170728
(311)http://www.findingdulcinea.com/news/on-this-day/June/Nelson-
Mandela-Sentenced-to-Life-in-Prison.html
(312) https://www.nelsonmandela.org/news/entry/historical-
documents-record-mr-mandelas-committal-to-prison

Alice VL

(313)https://www.sahistory.org.za/topic/umkhonto-wesizwe-mk-timeline-1961-1990
(314)https://www.newsmax.com/michaelsavage/winnie-mandela-necklacing-jerry-richardson/2018/04/02/id/852107/
(315) https://allthatsinteresting.com/necklacing
(316) https://www.theatlantic.com/international/archive/2011/09/south-africa-stands-with-qaddafi/244584/
(317)https://www.independent.co.uk/news/world/mandela-under-fire-for-failing-to-act-1581709.html
(318) https://www.biography.com/people/nelson-mandela-9397017
(319)https://www.sahistory.org.za/topic/sharpeville-massacre-21-march-1960
(320)http://www.un.org/en/events/mandeladay/court_statement_19 64.shtml
(321) https://www.sahistory.org.za/topic/umkhonto-wesizwe-mk
(322)https://franklin.library.upenn.edu/catalog/FRANKLIN_991873417 3503681
(323)https://www.news24.com/NelsonMandela/Speeches/FULL-TEXT-Mandelas-Rivonia-Trial-Speech-20110124
(324)https://www.theguardian.com/world/2001/feb/11/nelsonmande la.southafrica2
(325)   https://www.sahistory.org.za/people/winnie-madikizela-mandela
(326) https://www.bbc.com/news/world-africa-43627974
(327)https://www.sahistory.org.za/archive/statement-nelson-r-mandela-his-relationship-his-wife-13-april-1992
(328)https://www.nytimes.com/1997/12/04/world/winnie-mandela-s-ex-bodyguard-tells-of-killings-she-ordered.html
(329)https://www.theguardian.com/century/1980-1989/Story/0,,110268,00.html
(330) https://www.sahistory.org.za/people/thabo-mvuyelwa-mbeki
(331)https://www.news24.com/Africa/Zimbabwe/Mbeki-slams-US-barbs-about-Zim-20050222
(332)https://www.theguardian.com/world/2004/oct/05/southafrica.r orycarroll
(333) https://www.sahistory.org.za/people/jacob-gedleyihlekisa-zuma
(334)https://www.thesouthafrican.com/jacob-zuma-trial-a-history-of-jzs-legal-battles/

Alice VL

(335) https://www.bbc.com/news/world-africa-22513410
(336)https://www.reuters.com/article/us-usa-court-kavanaugh/senate-gets-fbi-kavanaugh-report-trump-rejects-democratic-criticism-idUSKCN1ME0Z1
(337)https://www.iol.co.za/news/politics/journo-forced-to-delete-pics-of-zuma-convoy-476604
(338) https://www.thesouthafrican.com/zuma-guards-attack-sa-and-uk-journalists/
(339)https://www.news24.com/southafrica/politics/hate-speech-charge-laid-against-jacob-zuma-20120224
(340)https://www.theguardian.com/world/2016/mar/31/jacob-zuma-ordered-repay-upgrades-nkandla-home-south-african-state-funds
(341)https://cdn.24.co.za/files/Cms/General/d/2718/00b91b2841d64510b9c99ef9b9faa597.pdf
(342) https://mg.co.za/article/2012-11-04-police-stop-zille-at-nkandla
(343)https://mg.co.za/article/2007-12-28-zuma-charged-with-corruption-fraud
(344)https://www.huffingtonpost.co.za/2017/09/14/its-been-a-long-road-and-president-jacob-zuma-is-almost-out-of-tricks_a_23209440/
(345)https://africacheck.org/spot-check/sa-president-jacob-zuma-charged-18-crimes-fraud-corruption-not-783/
(346)https://serve.mg.co.za/content/documents/2012/12/06/KPMG_report.pdf
(347) https://www.news24.com/SouthAfrica/News/more-tax-money-to-fund-jz-case-20180714
(348)https://www.timeslive.co.za/politics/2018-03-22-ramaphosa-explains-why-south-africans-are-paying-zumas-legal-fees/
(349)https://www.timeslive.co.za/news/south-africa/2018-08-15-police-were-not-provoked-when-they-shot-marikana-victims-iss/
(350)https://www.telegraph.co.uk/news/worldnews/africaandindianocean/southafrica/9501910/Striking-South-African-miners-were-shot-in-the-back.html
(351) https://www.sahistory.org.za/people/cyril-matamela-ramaphosa
(352)https://www.businesslive.co.za/fm/fm-fox/2017-09-07-ramaphosa-sex-scandal-the-little-story-that-couldnt/
(353)https://citizen.co.za/news/south-africa/1637683/ramaphosa-admits-having-had-affair-but-confessed-to-his-w
(354)https://citizen.co.za/news/south-africa/1637655/details-the-three-women-ramaphosa-allegedly-had-affairs-with/

Alice VL

(355)https://www.businesslive.co.za/fm/features/2018-03-16-nigerian-bank-investigation-could-embroil-mtn-ramaphosa/
(356)https://www.iol.co.za/news/politics/ramaphosa-makes-anthem-appeal-1725312
(357)https://www.news24.com/SouthAfrica/News/1-448-cops-have-criminal-records-20130814
ife-at-the-time-reports/
(358) https://www.bbc.com/news/10489457
(359)https://www.nytimes.com/2015/01/24/world/africa/jackie-selebi-south-african-police-head-convicted-in-corruption-case-dies-at-64.html
(360)https://africacheck.org/reports/south-africas-criminal-cops-is-the-rot-far-worse-than-we-have-been-told/
(361) https://csvr.org.za/docs/policing/tacklingpolicecorruption.pdf
(362)https://www.news24.com/SouthAfrica/News/27-crime-intelligence-officers-have-criminal-records-and-some-are-serious-20180528
(363)https://www.news24.com/SouthAfrica/News/10-cops-8-home-affairs-officials-arrested-for-extortion-20170329
(364)https://www.thesouthafrican.com/metro-cop-arrested-for-involvement-in-cash-in-transit-heists/
(365)https://www.news24.com/SouthAfrica/News/untouchable-cop-finally-suspended-20180418
(366) https://www.news24.com/SouthAfrica/News/ipid-explains-how-saps-captain-kgb-was-arrested-convicted-jailed-and-then-rehired-20180220
(367) https://ewn.co.za/2016/12/14/a-krugersdorp-cop-found-guilty-of-murder
(368)https://mg.co.za/article/2017-07-31-police-watchdog-cant-keep-up-with-crooked-cops
(369)https://www.telegraph.co.uk/news/worldnews/africaandindianocean/southafrica/11823852/South-African-police-officers-guilty-of-murdering-taxi-driver-Mido-Macia-by-street-dragging.html
(370) https://citizen.co.za/news/south-africa/653449/eight-cops-found-guilty-of-mido-macia-murder/
(371) https://www.iol.co.za/capetimes/news/traffic-officer-in-court-for-fraud-corruption-11955830
(372)https://www.news24.com/SouthAfrica/News/ct-traffic-cop-arrested-in-court-for-fraud-corruption-20171110

Alice VL

(373)https://www.iol.co.za/news/south-africa/limpopo/traffic-cop-who-allegedly-shot-at-teen-girls-charged-with-attempted-murder-15361988

(374)   https://citizen.co.za/news/south-africa/1756390/watch-they-took-a-r300-bribe-from-my-driver/

(375) ttps://www.arrivealive.co.za/news.aspx?s=2&i=33561&page=11-Traffic-officials-arrested-for-corruption-in-Mokopane

(376)https://www.telegraph.co.uk/news/worldnews/africaandindianocean/southafrica/11820945/South-African-police-officer-found-drunk-and-asleep-in-police-car.html

(377)https://www.news24.com/SouthAfrica/News/eden-park-police-station-robbed-r5-rifle-stolen-20180607

(378)   https://www.enca.com/south-africa/five-police-dead-in-attack-on-station

(379)http://www.conscienceradio.net/hillbrow-police-station-robbed-11-sleeping-duty-officers/

(380)https://www.iol.co.za/dailynews/cop-vehicle-abuse-out-of-control-in-kzn-14238043

(381)https://www.news24.com/You/Archive/photos-of-passed-out-pmb-cop-go-viral-20170728

(382) https://www.youtube.com/watch?v=07a4gRMT1Fk

(383)https://www.timeslive.co.za/sunday-times/lifestyle/2010-03-28-r14m-theft-of-cash-from-home-of-premier/

(384)https://www.timeslive.co.za/politics/2018-04-25-i-owe-guptas-nothing-for-airlifting-me-to-russia-dd-mabuza/

(385)https://www.news24.com/SouthAfrica/News/another-protection-order-against-dd-mabuza-20180512

(386)https://www.news24.com/SouthAfrica/News/mabuza-asked-about-mpumalanga-political-killings-20180320

(387)https://www.news24.com/SouthAfrica/News/mpumalanga-anc-denies-mabuza-has-a-private-army-20171206

(388)https://www.huffingtonpost.co.za/2017/12/19/the-5-ghosts-of-mabuzas-past_a_23312025/

(389)https://www.dailymail.co.uk/news/article-3121989/Widow-murdered-2010-South-Africa-Fifa-World-Cup-whistle-blower-Jimmy-Mohlala-says-husband-alive-today-hadn-t-exposed-multimillion-dollar-stadium-fraud.html

(390)https://www.huffingtonpost.co.za/2018/02/27/the-cats-out-the-

bag-who-is-deputy-president-david-mabuza_a_23371838/
(391)https://www.pressreader.com/south-africa/daily-
dispatch/20180531/281736975131516
(392)https://www.iol.co.za/business-report/companies/treasury-
backs-dan-matjila-15237963
(393)https://www.news24.com/SouthAfrica/News/anc-must-act-
against-defiant-mp-mondli-gungubele-mthembu-20170731
(394)http://www.politicsweb.co.za/news-and-analysis/da-lays-
criminal-charges-against-mayor-and-city-ma
(395)https://www.businesslive.co.za/rdm/news/2017-05-22-minister-
caught-in-sex-text-exchange-with-29-year-old-staffer/
(396)http://www.702.co.za/articles/312721/listen-the-spy-project-
that-funded-a-minister-s-r10-million-mansion
(397)https://www.msn.com/en-za/money/other/reports-r10m-secret-
state-spy-fund-used-to-buy-security-minister%E2%80%99s-home/ar-
BBKVKct
(398)   https://qz.com/africa/823517/fraud-charges-against-south-
africas-finance-minister-pravin-gordhan-dropped-the-currency-
strengthens/
(399)   https://www.reuters.com/article/us-safrica-gordhan/south-
african-state-prosecutor-drops-fraud-charges-against-gordhan-
idUSKBN12V0W7
(400)https://mg.co.za/article/2014-06-12-the-mystery-gigaba-bank-
account
 (401)   https://www.fin24.com/Opinion/connecting-the-dots-on-
gigabas-state-capture-project-20171009
(402)https://www.news24.com/SouthAfrica/News/download-the-full-
state-of-capture-pdf-20161102
(403)https://www.iol.co.za/sunday-tribune/opinion/lindiwe-sisulu-
political-legacy-propelled-by-principles-11756871
(404)https://mg.co.za/article/2014-03-16-sisulus-r11m-jet-bill-shows-
abuse-of-public-money-says-da
(405)   https://www.timeslive.co.za/politics/2013-04-28-menzi-
simelane-appointed-special-adviser-to-lindiwe-sisulu/
(406)https://www.news24.com/SouthAfrica/News/domestic-worker-
opens-fraud-case-against-mpumalanga-mecs-office-20170128
(407)   https://ewn.co.za/2015/04/28/Activists-call-for-Israel-travel-
bans-to-be-implemented
(408)https://mg.co.za/article/2011-06-28-land-expropriation-targets-

impossible-says-minister/%20
(409)https://www.news24.com/SouthAfrica/News/blade-nzimande-axed-as-higher-education-minister-20171017
(410)https://www.da.org.za/2017/06/sa-tourism-spends-r9-6-million-guptas-pr-agents/
(411)https://www.news24.com/SouthAfrica/News/water-dept-is-in-shambles-admits-nkwinti-after-taking-over-from-mokonyane-20180502
(412)   https://www.businesslive.co.za/bd/national/2018-03-08-nehawu-considers-reporting-mokonyane-to-hawks/
(413)https://www.iol.co.za/news/politics/ex-mec-abused-position-to-benefit-malema-1364643
(414) https://allafrica.com/stories/200303300087.html
(415)https://www.iol.co.za/news/south-africa/frustrated-skirt-lifting-minister-let-off-205996
(416)https://www.telegraph.co.uk/news/worldnews/1584731/Kill-the-criminals-says-South-African-minister.html
(417)https://www.dailymaverick.co.za/article/2014-08-26-marikana-commission-minister-shabangu-cant-act/
(418) https://www.news2
(419)https://www.iol.co.za/news/politics/zuma-downplays-malema-mantashe-spat-467742
(420)https://www.nelsonmandela.org/news/entry/the-fourth-nelson-mandela-annual-lecture-address
(421)https://www.africanews24-7.co.za/index.php/southafricaforever/gayton-mckenzie-sets-the-record-straight-on-zumas-poisoning/
(422)https://businesstech.co.za/news/energy/172931/minister-admits-south-africas-oil-reserves-were-sold-not-rotated/
(423)https://mg.co.za/article/2017-09-22-00-energy-minister-slips-up-on-oil-plan
(424)   https://mg.co.za/article/2018-01-16-the-board-still-has-to-consult-me-on-sabc-appointments-minister-kubayi-ngubane
(425)https://www.iol.co.za/news/politics/eff-warns-kubayi-ngubane-over-state-interference-in-sabc-appointments-12745134
(426)   https://www.pri.org/stories/2012-06-12/south-africa-police-chief-bheki-cele-fired-president-jacob-zuma
(427) https://allafrica.com/stories/201612080653.html
(428)http://www.politicsweb.co.za/party/this-is-nomaindia-mfeketos-

new-r8m-mansion--da
(429)	https://www.businesslive.co.za/bd/national/2018-03-22-da-wants-lindiwe-zulus-luxury-spending-on-two-bmws-investigated/
(430)https://mg.co.za/article/2013-07-15-thank-you-and-goodbye-cassel-mathale-resigns
(431)https://www.sapeople.com/2018/05/20/da-calls-for-cuts-as-ramaphosas-bloated-cabinet-costing-south-africa-millions/
 (432)	https://www.businesslive.co.za/bd/national/2018-05-28-trim-the-fat-ayanda-dlodlo-tells-her-colleagues/
(433)https://citizen.co.za/news/south-africa/292448/gender-payment-claims-unsubstantiated-protector/
(434) http://enacademic.com/dic.nsf/enwiki/11679839
(435) https://www.sahistory.org.za/dated-event/derek-hanekom-born
(436)https://www.sowetanlive.co.za/news/2017-04-08-dlamini-zuma-says-this-rubbish-anti-zuma-march-tweet-was-fake/
(437)https://www.timeslive.co.za/sunday-times/news/2017-10-29-gangster-republic-dirty-cigarette-money-is-funding-ndzs-bid-for-president/
(438)https://www.timeslive.co.za/sunday-times/news/2017-11-04-smoked-out-ndz-hanging-out-with-cigarette-smuggler-and-gambling-tycoon/
(439) https://mg.co.za/article/2006-10-16-travelgate-14-plead-guilty
(440)https://city-press.news24.com/News/dlamini-rejects-gordhans-social-grants-proposal-insists-on-keeping-cps-20170216
(441)https://www.reuters.com/article/us-safrica-welfare-court/south-africas-top-court-orders-end-to-welfare-grants-fiasco-idUSKBN16O1C1
(442)https://www.enca.com/south-africa/another-no-show-in-parliament-by-bathabile-dlamini
(443)https://www.msn.com/en-za/news/other/sassa-officials-fail-to-justify-millions-spent-on-security-for-bathabile-dlamini/ar-AAxFf5R
(444)https://www.news24.com/SouthAfrica/News/72-cops-to-be-charged-over-marikana-20170319-2
(445)https://citizen.co.za/news/south-africa/1417453/phiyega-misled-inquiry-on-her-role-in-marikana-massacre-must-go-claassen-report/
(446)https://ewn.co.za/2017/06/12/today-marks-end-of-phiyega-s-term-in-office
(447)https://www.iol.co.za/business-report/economy/zumas-r1-million-bribe-to-keep-minister-report-14076351

Alice VL

(448)https://www.news24.com/SouthAfrica/News/r1m-bribe-for-zuma-exposes-crisis-levels-of-abalone-poaching-da-20180325
(449)https://ewn.co.za/2017/12/07/da-opens-criminal-case-against-sfiso-buthelezi-and-lucky-montana
(450)https://www.facebook.com/Front-Nasionaal-SA-blad-743870385730868/
(451)https://www.news24.com/SouthAfrica/News/Dube-calls-for-lightning-probe-20110103
(452) http://www.digitaljournal.com/article/359996
(453)http://www.kickoff.com/news/40683/fikile-mbalula-slams-useless-bafana-after-chan-2014-exit
(454)https://www.pressreader.com/south-africa/cape-times/20131220/281513633974377
(455) https://www.youtube.com/watch?v=QFhWOuBiq6g
(456)   http://www.politicsweb.co.za/opinion/which-comes-first-the-anc-or-the-constitution
(457)
ttps://www.news24.com/SouthAfrica/Archives/ZumaFiles/Zuma-took-shower-to-reduce-HIV-risk-20060405
(458)https://www.news24.com/Archives/City-Press/Varsity-qualified-staffers-drain-SABC-Hlaudi-Motsoeneng-20150429
(459)https://www.pressreader.com/south-africa/citypress/20161030/281792808578160
(460)https://www.news24.com/SouthAfrica/News/we-want-the-rand-to-fall-so-that-when-it-rises-we-will-control-the-economy-maine-20161222
(461)https://city-press.news24.com/News/can-r753-support-a-family-of-5-bathabile-dlamini-thinks-so-20160621
(462)https://ewn.co.za/2014/01/09/Malema-slams-capitalism-praises-Mugabe
(463)https://www.iol.co.za/news/south-africa/eat-garlic-beetroot-and-lemon-manto-repeats-280721